NOW I'M CATCHING ON

NOW I'M CATCHING ON

MY LIFE ON AND OFF THE AIR

BOB COLE

with **Stephen Brunt**

PENGUIN

an imprint of Penguin Canada, a division of Penguin Random House Canada Limited

First published in Viking hardcover by Penguin Canada, 2016.
Published in this edition, 2017

1 2 3 4 5 6 7 8 9 10

Printed and bound in the United States of America.

Library and Archives Canada Cataloguing in Publication available upon request.

ISBN 978-0-14-319816-1
eBook ISBN 978-0-14-319815-4

www.penguinrandomhouse.ca

Penguin
Random House
PENGUIN CANADA

FOR MY FOUR CHILDREN,
CHRISTIAN, HILARY, MEGAN AND ROBBIE,
AND MY TWO GRANDCHILDREN,
GABRIELLE AND SAM

CONTENTS

FOREWORD

by Ron MacLean

"They may forget what you said, but they
will never forget how you made them feel."
—CARL W. BUECHNER

Hockey has become a sound Bob Cole makes.

In the 1993 playoffs, the Montreal Canadiens won ten consecutive overtime games on their way to capturing the Stanley Cup. During that run, Bob was chatting with Jean Béliveau about the Habs' remarkable overtime streak. Béliveau said, "You know, Bob, it's funny—I had a pretty good career, but I don't think I ever scored a goal in overtime." Bob, of course, corrected him, and Béliveau was pleased to hear that he had indeed notched one, and to discover the goal was scored in double overtime, but he was happiest to learn that it had happened during Bob's first-ever broadcast: April 24, 1969. They shared that story many times thereafter.

Bob has a defining call from every decade. In the 1970s it was January 11, 1976. The Soviet Red Army at Philadelphia, a very emotional game, as the Soviets were looking to humble the toughest team in the NHL. Who hasn't heard the recording of Bob announcing, "They're going home!" when it was clear the visitors had had enough? Bob stood by the Flyers and the NHL referee working the game, Lloyd Gilmour, and that sparked a trust between Bob and everyone affiliated with the league. Don Cherry often smiles about his respect for Bob, and he means it. Every time Bob came in to call a Boston Bruins game, Bob would insist on meeting Don one hour prior to the game to confirm Cherry's starting-line combinations. Now, Don had his own game-night ritual, which included taking a shower fifty minutes before the game and dressing while the players took part in the pre-game warm-up. But Bob was meticulous in writing out the lines. It took forever, and Don, realizing he needed to shower and get dressed, wanted to tell Bob to hurry up, but then he'd say to himself, Bob was there for us the day the Soviets tried to give the NHL a black eye—he can have all the time he wants.

In the eighties it was the Oilers' first Stanley Cup, May 19, 1984. "Folks! There's a new bunch on the block in the NHL." The Oilers adored Bob. The proof is that three of them were in St. John's for Bob's golf classic when Wayne Gretzky was traded on August 9, 1988. I can still picture Bob sorting out that crazy news with Kevin Lowe. Bob may own as many Wayne Gretzky sticks as the Great One himself. Don Cherry and I used to crack up as Bob would come around after a telecast with yet another Gretzky stick for his son, Robbie. Did Wayne not realize Robbie could open a shop with all the sticks?

In the 1990s Bob had many great calls of some exciting Toronto Maple Leafs teams, but his best call came during the '91 Cup final, May 17, Minnesota at Pittsburgh game two. Every hockey fan knows the goal—one of the most beautiful goals of all time, and certainly the most beautiful one-on-two. "Look at Lemieux. Oh my heavens, what a goal, what a move! Lemieux! Oh baby!" The final game of the series was game six in Minnesota, and the Penguins captured the Cup with an 8–0 victory. Don Cherry and I sat in the small dressing room we were using for a studio and watched the post-game celebrations with five Penguins players who hadn't dressed for the game. The Black Aces, as they're known. Happy for their teammates but envious and somewhat crestfallen. I still recall Bob showing up in the studio and giving them a pep talk about the unselfishness of their role in bringing about a winning team and about what the Stanley Cup ring and the stories from the dressing room would mean to their families, forever.

In the 2000s it's February 24, 2002, Salt Lake City, Utah. "Now after fifty years, it's time for Canada to stand up and cheer!" Joe Sakic had his Joe Carter "Touch 'em all, Joe—you'll never hit a bigger home run!" as exclaimed by the late Tom Cheek when Carter won the Blue Jays a World Series with a walk-off home run in 1993. In Sakic's case the audio loop, which still plays in his head, is "Gee-oooooh Sakic! That makes it 5–2 Canada! Surely that has got to be it!" Only Bob could turn the word "Joe" into a song lyric with two syllables, and give the whole country goosebumps.

In this decade, Bob's fire burned brightest in Montreal. "This is the playoffs . . . and this is Montreal!" Bob's work with Carey Price's brilliance stems from Bob's long-held belief, "Show me great goaltending and I'll show you a great hockey game." For six decades Bob has been the voice in the players' heads.

And mine, too. I came on the scene during the mid-1980s, pleased to share what I thought might be the twilight years of Bob's splendid career. Our dusk together has lasted thirty-one seasons and shows no signs of going dark. The above quote by Carl Buechner epitomizes how we all feel about Bob. It's not so much the selection or ordering of words, great as they are—it's the *emotion* of his play-by-play. It comes on you like smoke from a campfire. Warm, hypnotic, very much the spark of a story that will be passed on for years to come.

I have a personal recollection of getting that feeling from something Bob said. It was my rookie year with *Hockey Night in Canada*, 1986–87. I worked on a regional Toronto versus Chicago broadcast on a Friday night in Chicago for CHCH television, and then returned home to Toronto for the Toronto Maple Leafs *Hockey Night in Canada* telecast on the Saturday night. Bob walked into Maple Leaf Gardens at five-thirty and came into the studio, where I was having a cup of coffee, scanning game notes. Bob came right up to me and said in his minimalist way, "Watched the entire show last night in Chicago. Don't. Change. A. Thing."

I almost changed one thing. I stopped breathing. Nearly died right there and then. I battled a lot of anxiety in my youth. I was twenty-six years old when Bob said that to me. The feeling he gave me saved me. Throughout much of the first decade I knew him, I hung on every word Bob said.

After road telecasts our routine was standard. A group of us would hit the hotel bar and have a few drinks. Occasionally Bob would stop for one, but he likes Captain Morgan Dark rum, which wasn't available in most bars and never in the United States, so Bob preferred to just decompress in his room. I'd finish up with Don Cherry and Harry Neale, then go knock on Bob's door to see if he was game for a nightcap. Always.

Bob is a very slow and detailed drinker. He uses a tall glass, lots of ice, Captain Morgan, and Coke. (The original Coke.) He would pour the drink, and then not touch it for about twenty minutes. He would tell stories. Parables, usually. Instructing me on the ways of the industry, lecturing me on the purpose of our job. Bob was all about the game. Not the show, the game. And we would argue about that a fair bit, with me placing greater emphasis on show elements. Imagine the nerve of me. I can rationalize that it made for better drinking sessions.

Anyhow, after twenty or thirty minutes Bob would finally take a drink. He would down almost half the glass, and then set it aside for another half hour. I never got over his discipline. If we didn't have to work or fly the next day, we would sit and chat until the sun came up. Bob would look down as the streets of New York or some other large city came alive and we'd have one more to enjoy that scene.

Bob took me to Broadway productions. *Anything Goes* was his favourite. Bob's full of mischief. One day in Montreal, we walked into the movie *Red October*. It was a matinee and had just begun as we entered the theatre. Bob saw the Grand Banks on the screen and with his iconic voice informed everyone of the exact location of the filming, of the fish found at that particular spot in the Atlantic, and ended by telling folks to "come see Newfoundland and Labrador!"

Train rides, flights, hotel rooms . . . they were all schoolrooms in my life. From 1988 to 1994, every summer I would head to St. John's for Bob's golf tournament. Three days in early August. It never rained once. In 1989 Bob was in a pinch trying to get two more celebrities, so he phoned and asked me to find a pair in southern Ontario. I contacted Nelson Emerson and Rob Blake, two university kids from Simcoe, Ontario, who I knew would play in the NHL soon. They agreed to come down. Bob said, "Who in heaven's name is Rob Blake?" We have sure laughed about that over the years.

Bob always says, "I'm going to keep doing this until I get it right." He was taught early on by the very best: Foster Hewitt. Foster explained to Bob that you needed to work with four levels of emotional intensity. The first level was for scene sets and routine elements of the game. Level two was for important staging, a key faceoff, a power play, and moments within the game such as odd-man rushes. Level three was the big hit, or a really nice dipsy-doodle. And level four was for the goal or the save that was a difference-maker. You can hear and feel the four levels of Bob Cole. I was lucky to have Bob do for me what Foster did for him. We talked endlessly about work.

But it was on another stage that I discovered the most. That stage was his home. I know that the true secret to unlocking Bob's magic is to understand the real four levels of excitement in his life. Robbie, Megan, Hilary, and Christian, by name. The new bunch on his block. Bob's kids and now his grandchildren, Gabrielle and Sam, are the reason he has and will always offer us his level best.

INTRODUCTION

I remember exactly when I first came to fully appreciate the beauty and genius of Bob Cole's art.

Some years back, I was writing a book called *Gretzky's Tears*, which chronicled the trade that shook the hockey universe back in August 1988. Part of that exercise involved watching some of the highlights of Wayne Gretzky's remarkable career, including one that I remembered vividly: game seven of the 1993 conference final between the Toronto Maple Leafs and Los Angeles Kings, played at Maple Leaf Gardens.

If you're a Leafs fan, you don't need any reminding of what happened that night, or during that series. It was the closest Toronto has come to the Stanley Cup finals since their last victory in 1967.

Yes, the Leafs could have won the series in game six in Los Angeles, and maybe they would have if referee Kerry Fraser had seen Gretzky slash Doug Gilmour across the face and handed him the major penalty he deserved. But in game seven, with a Stanley Cup date versus the Montreal Canadiens hanging in the balance— now wouldn't that have been fun?—Gretzky carried the Kings to victory all but single-handedly. It was thrilling to watch, a singular night for arguably the greatest player in hockey history in the twilight of his career. But for Toronto fans, it was something else again. Looking down from the old Gardens press box, the sorrow in the building as those final seconds ticked away was palpable. It was as though you could feel thousands of hearts breaking all at once.

What I didn't hear, because I was there, was Bob's call of the game. Years later, while writing that book, I wanted to relive that game, and so I went out and found a recording of the *Hockey Night in Canada* broadcast. The dying moments of the third period were exactly as I remembered them, except now they came with a narration that perfectly mirrored the mood in the arena while also perfectly capturing what was taking place on the ice. It was so powerful and so precise that I sat down and transcribed every word and used it in the book. What the printed page couldn't convey, though, was Bob's performance, the subtle changes in tone and intensity that reflected what was happening. No actor could have done it better— and of course, actors almost always work from a script. Bob was improvising in the moment, taking what he saw in front of him, taking what he felt in the Gardens, keeping the basic narration going, the play-by-play, the names, and where the puck was and what was happening, but also conveying the emotional truth of that night.

Needless to say, that's incredibly hard to do, which I've come to understand all the better during my nascent broadcasting career. The more I think about it, the perfect comparison is what jazz soloists do when presented with a series of chord changes, with twelve or twenty-four or thirty-six bars: within that framework, they spontaneously compose their own melody from their imagination. Now, Bob would probably dismiss that analogy as way too pretentious (though as a lover of Frank Sinatra, he certainly has an ear for the phrasing and intonation of a great musician). But when you read the section of this book where he recounts his first conversation with Foster Hewitt about how to call a hockey game, how they discussed the idea of "feel and flow," how you're not just conveying information, but channelling the actual sense of a game to your audience—well, that's it, isn't it? And Bob learned that lesson better than anyone.

Ask hockey fans what they like about Bob Cole calling a game, and invariably the word that pops out is "excitement." He makes the game exciting, even when (sadly) the game itself isn't always all that thrilling. They're not all classics, they're not all blessed with miracle plays or dramatic tension or game-winning goals in overtime, but when Bob calls a game, your pulse starts racing when it should, you anticipate along with him, and if you're lucky enough to get an "Oh baby!" then you know you've witnessed something special.

Bob and I also share a great affection for the province of Newfoundland—he was born and raised there; I've been a part-time resident for the past fifteen years. And we're both avid Atlantic salmon fishermen, a pursuit that can be transcendent and maddening all at once.

I'm old enough to remember the Hewitts, Foster and Bill, broadcasting the Toronto Maple Leafs, and to remember the great Danny Gallivan when we were lucky enough to get one of the

Montreal games he called. As it is for many of us, though, Bob's voice is the hockey soundtrack of almost my entire life. All those great games, all those great moments, Stanley Cups being hoisted, Olympic gold medals being won. Wayne Gretzky's career from start to finish, and Mario Lemieux's. It's all Bob, for more than half a century. For Canadians, he has become like one of the family.

But there were also a whole bunch of things about Bob Cole that I didn't know before embarking on this project.

I didn't know about the childhood accident that almost cost him his leg, which led to him being confined to bed for months—and that it was there he first dreamed of doing play-by-play for hockey teams that he'd never seen in person, that were hundreds of miles away. I didn't know that as a kid he fell headfirst into a bucket of tar and almost drowned before being rescued by a passing stranger.

I didn't know that his father was the chief warden at the prison camp, or that Bob had crashed while piloting a plane and miraculously survived, or that he'd once done a barrel roll after being given control of a Snowbirds jet. I knew he curled in the Brier, but I didn't know that he got into an argument about curling with (of all people) Toe Blake. I didn't know that he once babysat Paulina Gretzky, or that he'd been involved in a street fight with a guy who may or may not have been a Mafia hitman, or that he'd had an Olympic radio broadcast ruined by Howard Cosell, or that he met Mickey Mantle at Yankee Stadium in 1956, or that Flip Wilson had once made it his personal mission to make Bob laugh—and failed.

It's been a remarkable life—even without the hockey part.

And it continues. Bob will be back calling games in the 2016–17 National Hockey League season. The word "retirement" isn't in his vocabulary. And now, when he works a game, social media explodes.

It would have been tough to explain to that kid confined to his bed in pre-Confederation Newfoundland, with his hockey cards laid out carefully around him, that one day he'd trend on Twitter, but no more mind-boggling, really, than telling him that one day he would be doing the same job as Foster Hewitt, that he'd be honoured by the Hockey Hall of Fame and receive the Order of Canada, that his voice would be instantly recognizable to millions of Canadians.

Yes, it's quite a story. What a privilege to help Bob put it down on the page.

Stephen Brunt
Hamilton, Ontario, and Winterhouse Brook, Newfoundland
2016

1

HOCKEY NIGHT IN
NEWFOUNDLAND

It was during the war years. Newfoundland was still a colony then, part of the British Empire. We didn't join Canada until 1949, when I was fifteen years old.

In St. John's, where I grew up, the school system and just about everything else was divided by religion—Catholics and Protestants. My father was a Roman Catholic and my mother was an Anglican, which made us unusual as far as St. John's families went. Pretty much everyone else was one or the other, but not both. Somehow my parents had worked it out after I was born and decided that when it came to school, I would attend Bishop Feild College, which was affiliated with the Church of England. That made me a Feildian. Our greatest rival was the big Catholic school, St. Bonaventure College, known to everyone locally as St. Bon's.

Football—that would be soccer to a lot of people—was our favourite game before the snow fell and the ponds froze. I especially remember a game when I was eleven years old, playing against St. Bon's down at the Feildian grounds. It was October or November. Even at that age, the competition between schools was fierce. I was a decent player then, they tell me, a good all-around athlete. And winning those games seemed like the most important thing in the world to me.

At one point there was a race for the ball. The St. Bon's keeper was coming out to get it, and I was running as fast as I could to beat him to it and score. It was going to be close. It was going to be me or him. And then there was a wicked collision. He came in low and took out my legs. I went down hard. Eventually, they pulled me up off the grass and put me down behind the goal. I remember the teacher who was there, Mr. Caines, coming up to me and saying, "Are you sure you're going to be able to get up, Robert?" I told him that I thought I was fine, and eventually I did get up, but I was down for a long time and my knee was very sore. I started walking home with a terrible limp. But the moment I got to the kitchen door, I had to make sure I wasn't limping anymore—otherwise my mother would be saying, "Here we go again. There'll be no more football for you!" So every day the limp would disappear when I got to the house, and it wouldn't reappear until I got around the corner and out of sight on my way to school. Then my knee would give out and I'd be hobbling again.

My leg kept getting worse. Finally, one day in January, I was coming home from school for lunch and was moving so slowly that I met the guys who were heading back for class—and I still hadn't made it to our house. I could barely walk, and the knee was badly swollen. I couldn't hide it from my mother anymore. She called our family doctor, Dr. J.O. Fraser, who came over to look at me that afternoon. He told me to get into bed and stay there. Three times a week he came to the house and used a syringe to draw fluid off my knee. It was bad enough that for a while, they thought I might lose the leg. I remember on one visit, my mother went off to speak with the doctor, and when she came back there were tears in her eyes. He must have given her bad news.

As it was, the leg was saved, but I wound up in bed from January to May—pretty close to five months.

People used to buy me model kits to put together to help pass the time. I loved making model airplanes, so I got a lot of those. I built them and hung them from my ceiling. Maybe that explains why I later got into flying.

My oldest sister, Helen, had a boyfriend at the time who owned a grocery store in the Battery—that's the neighbourhood that clings to the cliff right above St. John's harbour. He put up a notice in the store announcing that Robert Cole, a good little football player and hockey player, was bedridden, and asking if people would save their Quaker Oats box tops for me. If you saved up the box tops and mailed them in, Quaker would send you photos of the National Hockey League players. Eventually the whole neighbourhood was saving box tops for me, so I got all the pictures. That was unheard of. Nobody got all the pictures! I had all the Maple Leafs and Montreal Canadiens photos, plus a Leafs sweater, stockings, and a ring. I was in heaven.

Because we weren't part of Canada yet, we didn't have the CBC. The hockey games in those days were broadcast on Saturday night on the Newfoundland radio station, VONF, and then rebroadcast on

Wednesday afternoon. (I'd listen to the games in my room on Saturday night with all of my hockey photos laid out on the bed. No one was allowed to touch them. I had all the lines laid out, spread out down the bed and along the wall—Howie Meeker, Ted Kennedy, Vic Lynn, Gaye Stewart, and all the guys on those Leafs teams during and after the war. Syl Apps, the Leafs captain, was my hero.

When the game came on the radio, I was living it. Foster Hewitt made it sound like I was there. When Foster Hewitt said, "The Leafs are in the west end to my left . . ." I could see it, even though I'd never been to the Mainland, let alone Maple Leaf Gardens. He would paint a picture without you even knowing he was doing it. We talked about that when we first met years later. He told me, "You've got to paint a picture. You've got to bring that rink to the listener. *Kennedy takes it down the boards on the left wing. . . .*" And then he'd use his voice to tell the listeners how close the player was getting or how dangerous the situation looked. He'd go up and down octaves and get louder or softer. Some guys start out at full volume, but, as Foster explained to me, that's not the way to do it. Foster would build up the excitement, and he was really, really good at it.

Listening to Foster on Saturday night, with all my Leafs pictures out, or Montreal, if they were playing, it was like I had the game in my bedroom. And then on Wednesday afternoon, when the game was rebroadcast, I found myself remembering the words he'd used on Saturday. And now here I am imitating Foster Hewitt. My family got a kick out of that.

In May 1945, just after I was finally allowed to get out of bed, VE Day was declared: the end of the war in Europe. My sisters had saved up to buy me a bike to help get my knee going—a second-hand one, but new to me. I was riding it around and I saw the big party take over the streets. All the ships in the harbour were sounding their horns. Women were out beating on pots and pans. It was a huge celebration.

The next fall, I went back to school at Bishop Feild. Edgar House was our principal then. He somehow took a shine to me, even though I wasn't a great student, to be honest. Jeez, I didn't do homework often enough. All I really cared about was football and hockey. But he took to me and made me his helper in the chemistry lab and stuff like that. Mr. House also taught English grammar and literature, which I guess is why he had a wire recorder—the contraption that came along before the tape recorder. It was the first one I'd ever seen. He'd have us all take turns reading *Hamlet*, or something similar, and then play back the recordings so we could hear how we sounded. Elocution was a big deal in our school and I always got some parts to play. I never did go on to anything in the performing arts, but the voice was okay. I remember Mr. House saying, "Cole, you should think about a career in broadcasting." Funny how it all came together.

On Monday mornings when we arrived at school, the guys in the class would get me to do a bit of Saturday's game. I'd do the play-by-play for them, sounding like Foster Hewitt. And not just Foster. I'd do Wes McKnight as well, who was the host of *Hockey Night in Canada* in those days. "And now on behalf of Imperial Oil and Esso dealers everywhere, here's Foster Hewitt. . . ." I was talking to one of my buddies not long ago, who'd been a couple of grades behind me, and asked him if he remembered me doing that. "Jeez, yes," he said. "You did it all the time. Even when we were playing hockey down on the lake. You never stopped."

That's where it really started, in St. John's, capital of the colony of Newfoundland, spending five months in bed with a bad knee and a radio and Foster Hewitt and my hockey pictures and my imagination. It imbedded something in me. That's where I really began broadcasting hockey. I became passionate about hockey broadcasting then, and I still am today.

2

LIFE IN ST. JOHN'S

When I was a boy, we lived in a house on Quidi Vidi Road. (Some people like to pronounce it "kidee-videe," but for me it has always been "kwyda-vyda." That's what we called it then.) The place is still there, a row house, now painted a yellow colour, part of what they called Quidi Vidi Terrace. I remember we had six white lilac trees in the yard. Everybody had lilac trees then. And when I was a little fellow, I planted a maple in the corner of the yard.

It was a close-knit neighbourhood. Everybody knew everybody else. Belbin's Grocery was just down the block (it's still there—it's pretty popular now). I remember when Mr. Belbin was building the place. Three doors down from our house was St. Joseph's Catholic Church and the place where the priests lived. They had a guy who looked after the priests' house and he used to let me borrow his garden hose to wash my sister's car. The original church is gone now, replaced by a more modern building.

Out behind our house was a small field of gravel and grass. It's a parking lot now, but I can still show you where home plate was, and where the short right-field fence stood. I remember a ballgame when one of the neighbourhood guys, Billy Tracy, broke Mr. Green's window in the blue house a couple of doors down from ours. We all ran over behind where the hospital was being built and hid. But I said, "Guys, we've got to go back. Poor Mr. Green." So we went back and told him we'd fix the window and he was great about it. Then we continued the game. I was up. And didn't I hit and break another one of his windows. So off we went to the East End stores the next day. Everybody chipped in. A pane of glass cost about twenty-five cents back then—and we had to buy two of them.

In the summer, we played softball every night. We were more active than the kids today. There weren't enough daylight hours for us. I remember when Dad was home weekends, we'd play softball up behind the house and then we'd hear that voice. It would be dark and we could hardly see the ball, but we'd still be going because the game was tied. And I'd hear my father's voice: "Robert!" Then it was time. The game was over. No argument. Get in and get to bed.

My mom was a widow when she met my father. With her first husband she had three boys and then three girls. So she had six kids before she and my dad were married. Her first boy, born in 1912, was named Cecil. I'm named after him—that's my middle name. He was only six when the poor little fellow passed away. Apparently there was an awful fever. I remember going over to the graveyard as a kid and making sure that his little grave was tidy and the grass was cut. And then there was Kitchener—he died of tuberculosis at the age of nineteen. I was only nine months old when he died. And then came Edgar, and then Helen, Louise, and Olive—all a year apart, the three girls. Edgar went on to join the Royal Navy and served six years in the Second World War. Dad had two children from his first marriage: John and Margaret. I had many half-siblings.

Dad was a warden at His Majesty's Penitentiary. He had two children, a boy and a girl, before his first wife died and he met my mother. By the time I came along, his kids from his first marriage were on their own. So we had Mom and Dad, Edgar, and the three girls; then I was born, and my younger sister, Elinor. All of us lived in that little house. I don't know how we did it. Holy cow, there were only three bedrooms. I remember when I was a little boy, Mom and Dad's bedroom was also mine.

My parents were a bit older than most, which I guess was somewhat unusual for the times. Mom was forty when I was born and she had Elinor at forty-five. She had a tough time. My eldest sister, Helen, left school before graduating grade eleven because help was needed. She went to work outside the home, while the other two girls stayed in school. But you had to help out. With Elinor coming along when I was five years old, Helen was delegated to look after me. So it was a pretty busy place. I don't know how they did it, but somehow we all got everything we needed.

The other part that was a bit unusual was the mixed marriage. You have to remember that your whole life in Newfoundland in those days was determined by whether you were a Catholic or a Protestant. What school you went to, what teams you played for, sometimes even what stores you could shop in. In St. John's, the

Catholics were the majority, but the merchant class who ran most of the businesses, including the fishery, were mostly Protestant.

I guess the decision was made when my parents got together that we'd all grow up in Mom's church, the Church of England. My father's kids from his first marriage were Roman Catholics.

When Dad was home working in St. John's, he'd go to his mass at St. Joseph's. I was in the boys' choir at St. Thomas's, the Anglican church. He'd make sure I was ready for church.

"Get your boots shined and get going and don't be late. I'll be picking you up after church," he'd say. He'd pick me up and we'd go and visit his sister. That was the routine. And then we'd head down to Uncle Mart's on Sunday afternoon, and he'd have all his buddies there and they'd be playing cards, though at the time I didn't know what they were doing. Banging their hands on the table and rapping their knuckles. "Growl" is what they called the game. Or "A Hundred and Twenty." Ask any Newfoundlander and they'll know what I'm talking about.

Dad and his brother and sister were originally from a farming family. They owned a lot of the land around the head of Quidi Vidi Lake, where the Royal St. John's Regatta is held, the rowing races that also became a big part of my life. If you know where the old Memorial Stadium in St. John's was (it's since been turned into a Dominion supermarket), that was their land. When they were laying the cornerstone for that stadium, they brought in the figure skater Barbara Ann Scott, who'd just won an Olympic gold medal, to do the honours. I remember standing there with my dad during the ceremony.

The bridge at the head of the lake stood on land the Coles donated to the city. It was called the Cole Bridge until they replaced it a couple of years ago. There used be a plaque that went with it, but that's gone now, too.

Dad owned another section of property up along the shore of the pond, which he gave to his first son, Jack. Jack built a house there when he came back from the war and lived there until the day he died. He had spent the entire war, 1939 to 1945, with the Royal Navy. Funny to think that our family owned all that land.

Let me tell you a story about when I was a young boy—1939, so I would have been six years old—growing up in St. John's. Not far from where we lived on Quidi Vidi Road, the city council had an asphalt plant for fixing potholes and paving streets. Back in those days it was rather antiquated horse-driven stuff. In one area in the council yard were maybe a hundred forty-five-gallon drums of black tar. I was with another chap, who was a bit older than me—it seems I was always hanging out with older kids—and he was showing me how he could jump from barrel to barrel. They hadn't been opened, and it wasn't that far between them.

He was jumping and I was following, taking a different path through the maze of barrels. But it turned out that one of the barrels had its lid off. I saw it too late, in mid-air, and trying to stop myself, I guess, went headfirst into the tar.

So I was in it.

At that same moment, a guy happened to be walking by on the street—his name was Hubie Greaves. All he saw was a kid's boots sticking out of the barrel. He ran over and pulled out a little kid covered with tar—hair, face, eyes, ears, everything. He must have got my mouth cleaned out somehow. It's amazing what sticks in your memory. I can remember running home and feeling a burning sensation all over my body. I was scared to death. I had new coveralls and new boots and I knew that they were ruined. Mom wasn't going to like this. All the other kids on the street were running away from me. They saw this little boy coated head to toe in black tar screaming and running home. It wasn't far. Five minutes. I got in the back porch and Mom sent one of my sisters across the street to Walter Goss's grocery store and told her to buy all the blocks of butter she could find. She stripped off my clothes. I was bawling my eyes out and she was rubbing this butter all over my face and everything. And that got the tar off. I don't know how long it took to do all that, but it worked.

That was one of the stories I told my own kids when they were growing up—the day your father got stuck in the tar barrel. Now it's years later, and I'm down at the regatta with my three daughters, Christian, Hilary, and Megan (my son, Robbie, wasn't born yet). I always took my kids to the regatta just like my father did—and nearly every father does in St. John's. We were down by the bandstand listening to the music—the CLB battalion band always plays, and I love that. Then I saw a guy I recognized, Bern Penney, walking along the side of the lake down in front of us. He was a technician at the CBC when I worked there, and a veteran of the Second World War, but retired now. Bern waved at me to come down and introduced me to the guy he was with—Hubie Greaves. Yes, that Hubie Greaves. Except now he had a Scottish accent.

It turned out that after serving five or six years during the war, he married a Scottish lass and had lived in Scotland ever since. He was home on holiday to visit his sister. The tar barrel story happened just before he went off to war. Hubie remembered everything about that morning, and he told my daughters that it was a true story. "I saw these two boots sticking out and the other boy was crying out for help." So he pulled me out. And now there he was. Hubie Greaves, the man who saved my life. How about that?

AS I SAID, when I was a small boy my father's full-time job was as a warden of Her Majesty's Penitentiary in St. John's. My strongest memory of those days is from 1942, when the last hanging in Newfoundland took place. It was a fellow named Herbert Spratt, who had murdered his girlfriend. Dad was one of the witnesses for the hanging. I remember some friends and I climbed up the snowbank to look over the prison wall into the yard where they were building the scaffold. I asked my dad an innocent question about it and he scolded me pretty well not to talk about that anymore. I guess it was kind of tough on him. They brought in some guy from the Mainland to be the hangman. Nobody knew who it was. This is how they described it in the newspaper:

> At six o'clock yesterday morning, Rev. Father Power, of St. Joseph's, visited Herbert Spratt at the Penitentiary, and administered Holy Communion. The young man then went to the office of the Superintendent, where he wrote letters to his parents and to the family of the deceased girl, O'Brien. He thanked Capt. Byrne and the Attendants at the Penitentiary for their kindness. Officials state that during his time there, his conduct was exemplary. Yesterday morning he walked to the place of execution without wavering, and he was calm to the end.

Later, they asked my dad to find a location for a new prison they wanted to set up—a prison camp outside the city. He found a spot near Whitbourne, on a little island in Gull Pond on the Salmonier Line. (For you non-Newfoundlanders, that's on the west side of the Avalon Peninsula, about forty miles from St. John's.) The prison camp was still in operation until Premier Danny Williams got rid of it not that long ago.

For me, my dad's time running the prison camp was something else entirely. It meant he was only home on the weekends, so I didn't see him as much, except in the summer when we rented a cabin about ten miles from the prison and went up to visit him. But it also opened up a whole world of adventure for me.

The prison was a working farm. Everything was built by the prisoners, including the huge wooden bridge they used to get to the island. On the other side of the water they had a big vegetable farm—potatoes, turnips, cabbage, that kind of stuff. They grew it to feed the people in the hospital.

Of course, the chief warden's son got to do everything. I learned how to milk the cows and look after the piggery. But the best part was that the horses were mine.

I loved westerns. I knew all of the Lone Ranger stories. I read book after book. When I was bedridden all that time, I did a lot of reading. Your imagination could go wild with all that time on your hands.

So here I was at the camp, and they had two horses—farm horses. Big brutes. I was allowed to get up on the horses bareback and bring them back to the barn. That was a big thrill. The horses would lean down to get a drink of water and I'd almost fall off—they drank gallons. I rode the white horse for years up at the prison camp. And of course he was named Silver, like the Lone Ranger's horse. What else would he be?

There were some rough characters in that prison. Some of them arrived during the war or just afterwards, including some from England. They had a couple of murderers there, and some guys who were guilty of manslaughter. So it was a pretty heavy place.

My father ran a tight ship, I'll tell ya. He was a quiet-spoken man but very military sounding when he spoke. I can still hear his voice. "Robert." You jumped to attention pretty quickly when he was on the move.

I noticed that the prisoners responded in the same way. They respected him, and a lot of them really loved him. I'll tell you a story about that.

Years later, one of my buddies and I were out one night at the Bella Vista in St. John's, a place we used to go after hockey games to have a beer. We were sitting in a booth by ourselves when this guy came over to me and said, "You're Bob Cole, right? I'm going to buy you a beer. Can I sit down with you?" Now, you never want people jumping in. You don't know who they are. Well, he got us a beer and he sat down and he said, "I want to talk about your father."

Well, that's interesting.

"You wouldn't remember me, but I remember you when you were a little fellow. I used to serve you breakfast. And your dad did me a big favour."

He went on to tell me what a wonderful person my father was. It turned out that when Princess Elizabeth visited Newfoundland with Prince Philip in 1951, the chief warden could recommend a prisoner for a pardon.

"Your father wrote a letter and I got pardoned."

My dad apparently took a shine to this guy. His name was Walter Sweeney, and he was serving twenty-five years to life for murder. They still say he didn't do it. I don't know much about the details of that. When he was at the prison camp he was selected by dad to be the steward in the wardens' residence—the big house where the five or six wardens lived. And now here was Walter Sweeney talking to me years later. I'll be danged.

3

THE BOUNDING MAIN

I guess it made sense that I would fall in love with ships. St. John's is a port city, and life there has always centred around the harbour. The house I grew up in was just a short walk from the wharves. All the kids used to hang out down there, watching the ships come and go—freighters, fishing trawlers, the white fleet that came from Portugal every season to fish. But I loved the passenger ships. There was something almost mystical about them. The RMS *Newfoundland*. The RMS *Nova Scotia*. Big passenger ships owned by the Cunard Line, painted to look like the *Queen Mary*. The *Fort Amherst*. The *Fort Townshend*. Sailing off to New York and who knows where. I loved to imagine where they might be headed.

I had a buddy named Jimmy Young. We played football together through junior high and into high school. He was a great outside left and I was inside left. We were really close on the pitch and off, sleeping over at each other's houses. His father had an important role with

Harvey and Company, who were the agents for the *Fort Amherst* and *Fort Townshend*. I told Mr. Young a couple of times that I'd love to go to sea someday, but I was never sure if he took me seriously. Then one Saturday morning, Jimmy phoned me at home and said that his dad wanted to know if I still wanted a job on a ship. Of course I did. "Well, you'd better come down to the wharf," Jimmy said, "Pier One down at Harvey's. They're looking for a bell boy."

School was out for the summer. I was sixteen years old and had never set foot outside Newfoundland. So I went down and met Mr. Young and he took me aboard the *Fort Amherst* and introduced me to the chief steward. "Good-looking young boy," he said. "Does your mother know you're here?"

"Yes, sir," I said. That was the first lie.

"We're sailing in three days," he said. "You have to get some pictures taken. You have to get your passport done and pick up your merchant seaman papers. And you'll need a white shirt and black trousers."

I didn't ask any questions. But I had a job. I was going to sea.

What a scramble. My sisters chipped in to get everything going. My sister Louise's boyfriend, Eddie Ringman, was a photographer who worked at Holloway Studios. We went over there and got the pictures taken and the passport was done in half an hour.

Three days later, I was sailing through the Narrows into the North Atlantic. My whole family was out standing on the rocks in the Battery waving as we left the harbour. I was on the afterdeck watching. Off I went—and I didn't even know where I was going. I was the youngest on the ship.

There were 180 passengers in first and second class. First class was pretty fancy—three-course meals every day. Halifax was our first stop. New York was our second—Pier 95. I'll never forget it. The first morning I woke up in New York, there at the next dock to our starboard side was the *Queen Mary*. What a thrill for a young boy getting away for the first time in his life. I grew up in a hurry, I'll tell you.

So what's a bell boy, you ask? It's not like in a hotel. Back then, in the ship's kitchen there was what was called a bells board, which had rows of different bells. Each bell represented one of the ship's officers—the captain, the first officer, the chief officer, the chief engineer, the doctor. They all had their own signal. So when their bell sounded and that red light came on, I'd take off to wherever the bell had been rung and get whatever they wanted. Usually in the afternoon when we were sailing, they were calling for another bucket of ice.

Your job became your nickname on the ship. You didn't go by your real name. I was "Bells." "Bells, get this." "Bells, get that." All of the stewards on the ship had a chore. They were called scrub downs. Every morning before the passengers got up—and we had a couple of hundred passengers—I had to get up at 6:30 am, get in my fatigues, and scrub down the Captain's quarters on the third deck, including all of the stairway outside and down to the next deck and all of that stuff. It had to be spotless. After, I'd change into my uniform—white jacket, black trousers, and bow tie—have breakfast and be ready for my bell boy chores.

I also delivered the news every morning. I got a real kick out of that. I'd go to the radio officer's quarters in the aft end of the ship where they had the wireless and collect copies of the news of the day. There were no telephones on the ship. No outside connection for the passengers. It was me. The captain got his news first and then the chief officer and the doctor and the rest of them. Then I had a series of places where I'd take copies, going around the ship and pinning the news of the day, including sports news, on to the notice boards of each deck. As a baseball player at home and a hockey player, I was a big sports fan. The one summer I worked on the ship was 1951 when the New York Giants and Brooklyn Dodgers had their famous pennant race—the one that ended with Bobby Thomson's "shot heard 'round the world" when the New York Giants overtook the Brooklyn Dodgers and won the World Series. I was all decked out in my uniform telling everybody about that. Whether they were fans or not, they became fans. Every morning it was a big deal when I came around and told them what happened the day before in the major leagues. It was great.

Before we sailed, they gave me this little xylophone-type thing, which had four notes. Part of the bell boy's job was to march around the ship when we were ready to sail and announce, "All ashore, everybody. Sailing in half an hour." I played the bugle in the CLB band back home and, lo and behold, the xylophone played the same four notes as a bugle. All I had to do was hit the thing—*ding, ding, ding*—to get people's attention. But I improvised a bit. When we were ready to sail I could play, "Sailing, sailing, over the bounding main. . . ." So I was a hero. "Who's the new bell boy?" people kept asking. It worked out pretty good.

When we landed in New York, we had three days before we sailed again. I found out that the first officer was a friend of the Toppings, the Yankees owners. I told him what a Yankees fan I was and he arranged to get me a ticket to Yankee Stadium. I went up to the Bronx by myself on the subway, found my way to the stadium, and looked around outside before going in. I saw some nice cars parked there. They had to be players' cars, I figured. After the game I waited there and didn't I meet Tommy Henrich on his way out of the park. His was the first autograph I ever got. And then Phil Rizzuto came out and we had a little chat. Oh my God, I was in heaven.

From New York, we set out on a twenty-three-day cruise through the Caribbean. I can still remember the stops: St. Thomas, St. Kitts, St. Croix, St. Lucia, Martinique, Guadeloupe, Grenada, Barbados, Trinidad and Tobago. Finally, we hit a place in Venezuela for just a few hours, and then headed back through the islands to New York.

We landed in Barbados and were given a couple of hours off. Some of the other guys on the crew said, "Bells, we're going ashore and we're taking you with us."

All I wanted to do was get on the beach and see what the white sand was like and the blue water. Can you imagine? I'd never been away from home, and Newfoundland may be an island, but it's nothing like that. But the boys had other plans for me. They were all dressed to the nines—the stewards always dressed well. We went to this place called The New Yorker. We walked in and went up the stairs and on our way passed all these ladies on the rails. I remember I was actually scared. They would touch your arm or your shoulder as you went by. I didn't like the place at all. I'd never heard of drinking in those days—kids of my age just didn't do it. And I wasn't going to start there. (I didn't have my first beer until I was twenty-four or twenty-five years old.) When we got upstairs this lady came over and sat next to me and talked and talked and talked. The guys kept disappearing, and I didn't know where everybody was going but they were gone.

A few years later, I figured it out.

I had another memorable experience when we were docked in Trinidad. I had some time off and went off on my own to the local country club. It was a beautiful, jungly looking place with thick-growing trees and cages housing animals. One little monkey caught my eye. There was a rail from where I was standing down to his cage. The cage was open and he had a chain on his foot that kept him from running away. The monkey could walk up that rail to the people who were standing there. A sign on his cage read, "Please Don't Feed the Animals," but I ignored that. I had a piece of banana and I thought that monkey was cute. He came up and looked at me and was actually smiling. I reached out and tried to give him a tickle, like you would with a dog or something. Why, that little son of a gun grabbed my finger in his teeth so fast. Jeez, you talk about getting a scare. And it hurt, too. It was like he was going to chew it off. All by myself, in Trinidad, what am I up to? I'll never forget the face on him. Man, I hated that monkey. . . .

ON SOME OF the smaller islands in the West Indies we didn't go to a dock but would anchor just offshore. A pilot ladder ran down the starboard side of the ship, and passengers and crew would climb down it to the boats that came to take them to and from the island. There was one island where I didn't go ashore. I decided I'd put my swimming gear on and go down the pilot ladder—it had a bit of a platform when you got past the steps, like a small landing—and dive into the lovely warm water and have some fun. Right after I got in, one of the guys on the upper deck started shouting, "Bob, there's fins in the water out there!" I wasn't a great swimmer but I hustled back. Now the tide had lifted the ship a few feet. I couldn't reach the ladder. I was a little panicked before I finally grabbed hold of it. I sure learned a lesson.

We docked the ship at the next island two or three days later. The local kids came out on the wharf and dove in the water for quarters that the passengers threw. Some of the island folks came on board the ship with a steel band, and some stood up on the rail on deck—it's a long way down from there—ready to dive for the quarters.

We watched one youngster, all of fourteen years old, dive off the rail and go down under the ship, under the keel, and up the other side. It was astounding athleticism. Later, when I was going for a swim off the side of the boat, I decided to try to see if I could get down to the keel and up the other side. I filled my lungs as much as I could and headed down.

The ship's side was going straight—no sign of the curve of the hull. And I'm looking at it, swimming hard, and it's still straight. It hasn't even bowed in yet and I'm almost out of breath. I finally figured out I'd gone too far and I was never going to make it. Now, I don't mind telling you this—I barely made it back to the surface. What a stupid thing to be doing.

I guess I was daring. Trying things that I shouldn't be trying. That may explain the tar barrel thing. Whatever seemed to be impossible I tried to do. That's my makeup. Reaching for the top—that's what I was doing.

THE TRIP FROM St. John's to New York, through the Caribbean and back, took forty-two days. On the way home, some of the guys in the crew took me ashore in New York and told me they were going to get me dressed up. They took me to 42nd Street where all these clothing stores where they seemed to know everybody. I got decked out in a corduroy jacket and a brand new this and a brand new that. I came home to St. John's dressed to the nines in clothes out of New York. I learned later that the boys had taken me to the place where they bought all their stuff—it was good stuff but it was second-hand. I didn't know that. They were brand new suits to me. They looked pretty sharp.

That summer, I made enough money to pay my tuition at Bishop Feild. It was a big help to Mom. We didn't have too much then.

The next year, the *Fort Amherst* was back in St. John's for three days, loading passengers and freight. I went down just to visit the guys. The chief steward called me over and said, "We've got an opening in the first-class saloon. It's yours if you want it. We're sailing the day after tomorrow." I wound up working as a steward in the main dining room, so that was pretty high class. That summer we did exactly the same route. All the same islands. Even today, that route is still vividly imprinted in my mind. It was a dream job.

4

THE PATH NOT TAKEN

The first time I saw a professional hockey game in person was the spring of 1949. In those days, National Hockey League teams that missed the playoffs sometimes went on barnstorming tours to make a few extra dollars (that tells you how much hockey players made back then). That year, the New York Rangers finished dead last in the standings, and they headed out to the Maritimes. I remember reading about it in the St. John's *Daily News*. The Rangers were doing a tour, and the one stop in Newfoundland was going to be in Grand Falls, the only place in the province at that time with a regulation-sized ice surface.

In those days, we all learned how to handle guns, and I had done some rifle shooting with the Royal Canadian Air Cadets. It was a big part of growing up. At some point I had managed to buy myself a Remington rifle. I sold it to pay for my train ticket to Grand Falls on the old Newfoundland railroad. I think it cost twenty-five bucks.

The year before, I had been in Grand Falls playing with the senior intercollegiate team from Bishop Feild. We were billeted in different places, and I stayed with a family, the Bartletts, who ran a big farm near Grand Falls. I called them and asked if I could I stay with them for a night. I didn't have any money other than what I'd spent on the train ticket. Luckily, they agreed to take me in and so I headed off to Grand Falls.

When I got there, I went downtown and found the Rangers (Grand Falls is a small place). I met heroes like Allan Stanley and Gus Kyle and Chuck Rayner. I'd gone to heaven. This was my first taste of the pros, and they were all so good. I brought the Brownie camera and took some pictures—I've still got them somewhere. It was fabulous, seeing the New York Rangers in those beautiful uniforms. I don't know if people today could ever understand what that meant to a youngster in Newfoundland back then, to meet those players. Allan Stanley was talking to me. Crazy. I couldn't believe it.

They played against a senior all-star team. George Faulkner, the brother of NHL player Alex Faulkner, was on the team. George was from Bishop's Falls just down the road and was an up-and-coming star. They had some good imports from places like Kirkland Lake, too, as well as some guys who'd been brought in to play for Buchans, the Newfoundland mining town, or who'd come to work in the paper mill in Grand Falls. There were some good hockey players in that game. I'll never forget it.

Some years later, in 1956, the Boston Bruins toured Newfoundland after they missed the playoffs. Gerry Regan, who was in Prime Minister Pearson's Cabinet and later became premier of Nova Scotia, was the guy behind that tour. The Bruins played a lot of games in Newfoundland that year, taking the train right across the province, stopping in Corner Brook, Grand Falls, Bay Roberts, and Gander, as well as St. John's. They played the Bay Roberts game on an outdoor rink—that's the one that ended with all twenty-three members of the Conception Bay team on the ice at the same time against the Bruins. And that's the game where goalie Terry Sawchuk took the puck and skated the length of the ice and scored a goal.

I was playing with the Feildians, the senior team, and working at radio station VOCM, and I was picked to be part of the team that played against the Bruins at the stadium. It was a fun thing. I mean, these were the Boston Bruins.

Fleming Mackell and I got to be buddies quickly—he was a great centre for the Bruins, an All Star, and before that he'd been on a couple of Stanley Cup–winning teams in Toronto. Fleming was the one who helped me to meet the guys. I took my tape recorder down to the Newfoundland Hotel, and I got all the guys to record little promos for my broadcasts on VOCM. "This is Doug Mohns of the Boston Bruins. Tune in to Bob Cole tonight on VOCM. . . ." Stuff like that. They were all great.

Not many people got along easily with Terry Sawchuk, but I can tell you that I did. In fact, I lent him my car while the team was in St. John's—a '51 Chevy. He took it wherever he wanted to drive, and that was fine with me.

The game was a lot of fun. Mackell and I set things up so we staged a fight. I can't even remember how many goals were scored, but I remember the guys—Fern Flaman, who was the captain,

Lionel Heinrich, Johnny Peirson, Cal Gardner, Bob Armstrong, to name a few.

When they were getting on the train to leave the next day, Sawchuk came up to me and asked me why I'd asked all the other guys to record a promo but not him. I guess I must have missed him when he was out driving my car.

I didn't have my tape recorder with me, but wouldn't that have been great?

FLYING WAS ALWAYS grabbing at me. Maybe it comes from growing up during the war years. I built model airplanes and always hoped that someday I would have a chance to fly. As soon as I could, I joined the Air Cadets. I knew that they had a program where, if you did well, they would send you to flight school. So I studied hard and got some help and wrote the exams. Every year they'd award two hundred scholarships across Canada. I made the cut. I didn't know if I was number two hundred or number one. It didn't matter. I was in there somewhere. The commanding officer called me one day and said I had won a scholarship, and that I'd be heading for Yarmouth, Nova Scotia, to learn to fly. That was a home run.

I had just turned nineteen. There were fourteen Air Cadets from Nova Scotia, New Brunswick, and Newfoundland. You studied and took flying lessons, and when you soloed successfully, you got your wings automatically. The idea was to encourage us to join the air force—and that was my plan all along. I was sponsored by the Kinsmen Club back home to get a private licence, which would require another fifteen or twenty hours of flying. By the end, I'd be able to fly, but I wouldn't be able to get paid for it yet. For that you needed a commercial licence.

Gerry McKay was our instructor. He had been a Spitfire pilot during the Second World War, so immediately he was my hero. What a lovely guy, too. We were flying out of the Gateway Flying Club.

I was the first one in our group to solo—in a little over three hours. Usually it takes around eleven or twelve. I'll never forget that day. We went up, came back and landed, and then Gerry turned over his shoulder and said, "Can you take it around yourself?"

"Do you think I can?" I asked him.

"That's not what I asked you, Bob. Do you think you can take it around yourself?"

I said, "Yessir."

He got out and he left me in the airplane with my heart pumping like you wouldn't believe. Oh jeez, what a thrill. Your first solo. Talk about a powerful feeling. You're alone. You look at the tower— we didn't have radio to the tower then—and you wait for the green light. He gives you the green light, then you wave to him and you take off. You know what you're doing, your climbing rate, you turn left, then downwind, then that first landing. What a feeling.

I was looking forward to my first solo cross-country flight. I told Gerry I wanted to fly to Greenwood Air Force Base because a lot of cadets from Newfoundland were at camp there, and I wanted to be a hero to my friends. It wasn't too far away. I was just kidding him. He said, "No, you're not going to another airport. You're going to do a triangular cross-country course. I'll pick the spots that you must identify. You'll take off from here and come back here."

I always wondered if he was thinking about that conversation the day I went off for that first solo cross country flight . . . and didn't come back.

The plane was a Piper J-3 Cub. I was flying along at three thousand feet and everything was going smoothly. Then I got to the spot where I had to identify this summer shed and turn there and do the other part of the triangle back to the airport. I made the turn and looked down at my instrument panel and noticed that I was losing RPMs. I added a little more power, trying to get the RPMs up to where they should have been. But they kept dropping, and I couldn't figure it out. Later it was explained to me that it was a hot day and the carburetor had started icing. But I didn't know that at the time. I decided to drop down five hundred feet, turn back to the other point of the triangle, and then head home. But I always liked having fun when I was flying. I loved aerobatics. So I wasn't just going to glide down. I was going to do a stall, and maybe do a spin. I put her nose up and cut the throttle. I was waiting for the air speed to drop back so I could stall her and do the spin. And just when I got up so far and she was ready to stall, the propeller stopped dead.

You start those airplanes from the outside by throwing the propeller, so there was no way to restart it. Jeez. That was a big fright.

There's a rubber handle on the stick of a J-3. It's like a little trigger that's shaped for your fingers. It came off in my hand. I must have really panicked. But then I gathered my thoughts. Held the stick back. Kept her level in a gliding mode, and just like the book says in a situation like that, looked right away for a place that might be conducive to putting an airplane down. All I could see was woods and water. I wasn't going to put it in the water. But I saw what looked like a clearing down there in the woods. I was still at three thousand feet, so I couldn't be sure. But I had to make up my mind, and I decided that this was where I was going.

Then I started going through an emergency checklist, just the way we'd studied it. Make sure that everything is harnessed down. The fire extinguisher is fastened, your seat belt is fastened. Check everything again. Is there any possibility of starting the airplane? No. Check the winds—I'm going to land into the wind. Everything is working pretty good. I've kept a clear head. And now . . . I'm going to crash. I do a little weaving back and forth, get lined up into the wind, and get into the final part of the descent. And I notice that the clearing doesn't look so clear after all. Jeez, this is not too good. But I'm committed. This is where I'm going.

There was a huge rock at the near end of the clearing. And at the far end there were two big strong-looking pine trees. They were almost perfect for going between. I had to be very lucky to be at the perfect height, and I was. I was going to land right between the two trees. I hit the right one a second before the left one so the airplane went *bang, bang* and she came to rest nose down.

The glass in the cockpit was broken. I was sitting there waiting for the pain to hit me—and nothing. Just a little bump on the head and a small cut somewhere. Wow. I'm down. It's quiet. Not a sound. So I opened the door and got out and gathered myself. I guess I started laughing or something. I looked at the airplane. The two wings were broken. But the engine and the prop were perfect. Didn't touch 'em. The wheels were stuck down. They didn't retract. I'm safe. I'm out.

Now the book says stay with the airplane. Don't leave the airplane. Don't start walking when you don't know where you're going. I tried to figure out where the sun was—okay, that's west. I didn't quite know where I was but I knew where west was and I knew Yarmouth was west somehow, but I wasn't going to walk. I stayed put.

I was a smoker back then. I had a pack of cigarettes and no match. So I did the Boy Scout thing. I got some little twigs, some pieces of dried leaves, and tried to make a spark. I'll tell you, I'd like to see someone start a fire by rubbing two sticks together because I sure couldn't do it. I got them hot but I couldn't get a spark. So no cigarette.

It turned out I was well in the bush not far from a place called Kemptville, Nova Scotia. I'm not back yet, I'm overdue. Now everybody is getting worried. The news started to circulate in Yarmouth that they'd lost a cadet. It would have been a disaster for the flying club, which was in financial trouble. This would be a bad thing to happen—to lose a boy. The tower in Greenwood was contacted and soon they had airplanes up. I saw them from the ground sitting by my plane. They were going back and forth, but they were too far away.

The way they found me was really something. Trans-Canada Airlines, or TCA—which eventually became Air Canada—had a flight going from Yarmouth to Halifax, a Douglas DC-3 Dakota flown by a pilot named Bob Franklin. After I was lost, he had been told to keep his eyes open. He came overhead and must have seen this oblong thing in the woods. He got permission to circle back and, jeez, he came so low. He banked right around me and I was waving and waving. I could see him in the cockpit.

They later wrote an article about it in *Between Ourselves*—the TCA magazine—and had a picture of Bob Franklin on the cover. I remember it said, "The sharp eyes of a TCA captain rescues young pilot. . . ." He circled overhead and called the Yarmouth tower to tell them he had seen the wreckage, and that it appeared the young man was fine. He was waving at me. He got permission to stay there for a few more circuits until they spotted me. The passengers were having a ball. They were all over on that side of the airplane looking. I saw their heads in the windows. Jeez, I'm saying, somebody do something, and get me out of here. . . .

Of course, everyone back in Yarmouth was delighted when I was found alive. Not only that, I saved the engine, saved the prop, saved the crankshaft. Gerry jumped in the Piper Pacer with the president of the flying club, who was a doctor, and they flew out to where the TCA pilot had pinpointed my location. He came down so low—he was a Spitfire pilot, remember—that I could see his face. Then I saw them throw something from the airplane. Great, I figured maybe this was matches and supplies. It took me fifteen minutes to find it in the brush and Gerry was still circling. I waved to him to let him know I had it, and he left. He dropped that frigging thing and he left. It was a little piece of metal he must have found in the cockpit of his airplane with a note tied to it. And all it said was, "Stay with the airplane all night if necessary. We'll be back." That's it.

It's starting to get dark now. I know it's bear country around there. And don't I start to hear frigging bears. The snorting and low growling. So I got in the airplane and I couldn't get to sleep because she was on kind of an incline. I closed that little Plexiglas window and thought, "That's not going to stop a bear if he comes." So I got out of the airplane and I stood there. It was pitch-black and about three in the morning when I finally heard voices calling out. It was one of the cadets from St. John's and another one from Halifax. Some farmer took them in his truck as close as he could get them to where I was and they came the rest of the way on foot. So it was a pretty good search party. The first thing I heard was, "Bob, are you all right?" Then we were all hugging each other. They put a bandage on my forehead where it was cut. We hiked out and got in the truck and the farmer drove us back to the flying club at the airport.

The next day was foggy and there was no flying. The following day we reported for breakfast in the morning. The fourteen cadets lived at the end of one of the runways in what had been the commanding officer's home during the war. Gerry arrived and said, "Coley, come on, you're up." I was the first one he called. Holy cow. I figured I was maybe going to be sent home for cracking the airplane up and the rest of it. But they were all pleased that everything turned out the way it did and I didn't get hurt. It turned out to be good. And he was going to take me right back up.

Gerry said, "You take her off." So I took her off and I was shaking like a leaf and couldn't stop. He knew that. And then he said, "Level off at two hundred feet." Level off at two hundred feet??? Two hundred feet is just over the trees. To that point, I hadn't done any low flying. We skimmed over fir trees all over the outskirts of the airport in Yarmouth. Eventually, the shaking stopped and I was okay. I wasn't nervous. He got me out of it and that was it. I was fine after that.

I was tidying up my desk the other day and I found this newspaper article—"Young Air Cadet Crashes Airplane." It's a funny thing.

Everybody is different, I guess, in the way they remember things. When I think back to the crash, I'm mostly pleased that I reacted sensibly.

IN THE END I didn't wind up enlisting in the air force. A buddy and I went down and saw the recruiting officer. I had the Air Cadet flying scholarship, so that's an in to becoming a pilot. That must be what they want you to do. But the recruiting officer said, "You'll go in as air crew. You'll serve one year as training and then five years committed to the air force. So it's six years." That was fine with me because I wanted to fly. But then he said he couldn't guarantee me flying. "Air crew" could be a navigator, a radio operator, anything. He said, "You've got your private licence through the Air Cadets. You're probably going to be selected for pilot training. But I can't guarantee it." In other words, I was taking a chance. I didn't want to be a navigator. I understood what he was saying. There may have been too many on the course that year or something. Maybe I'd be better as a radio operator. But I didn't want that. I got cold feet. I said no. And I didn't do it.

But I did keep flying recreationally. In St. John's you could rent a plane for eight dollars an hour. Every chance I'd get, I'd rent an airplane and go flying. Which reminds me of a story, and another newspaper headline: "Young Pilot Wins Bombing Contest."

I had a friend from school, he was in the class ahead of me, a good football player, named Hubert Hookey. He was interested in going flying with me, so I told him the next Sunday, we'd go.

We were both out of school and working by then. I rented an airplane for Sunday afternoon and had Hubert with me and we were going to go up for half an hour—it would cost four bucks. But the club said they couldn't rent me the plane. They had a bombing contest going on for all their members. You couldn't take a plane unless you went in the bombing contest. Now, I didn't want to go in a bombing contest. I just wanted to go up and show my friend the harbour. But they wouldn't let me do that. They told me I could take the plane for half an hour, but I had to enter the contest. I had no choice.

So they explained it to me. "You take off and you circle out there and you'll see a giant X in a circle between runway twenty-five and twenty-nine. You've got to go to a thousand feet." They gave me three bags of plaster of Paris and said to just throw them out of the plane and try to hit the target.

Up we went. I told Hubert we'd get the bombing part over first and then go for a spin around the harbour. We climbed up to a thousand feet and circled against the wind. I slowed the airplane down as much as I could.

I said to Hubert, "I'll tell you what I'm going to do. I'm going to cut the throttle a little bit and when I say 'throw it,' you throw it out the window."

(Years later, I was with my family and we met this little girl after a church service on Christmas Eve. She said, "Mr. Cole, I'm Hubert Hookey's daughter. We always laughed about the time you took him flying. You frightened the life out of him.")

I cut the throttle to slow her down and when I got to where I thought the big circle was, I turned her up pretty straight. So now Hubert's looking straight down at it. He let the bag go.

I said, "Now we're going to circle around and do another one."

By that time I'd got the airplane moving pretty good. Off a steep turn, now level, now a left turn again.

"No, I'm not throwing another one," Hubert said. "I'm not doing it." He was fastened to his seat. I didn't know what was wrong with him.

So I said okay, I'll do it myself. I went over, banked, opened my window and threw the second bag, turned again, passed over the X again, opened my window, banked, and threw the third one.

Thank God we got rid of that shit. And Hubert's still sitting there petrified. I took him for a little ride down around the harbour. It was a nice half hour. Then I landed the airplane and came in.

When I taxied into the flying club, Pete Rendell, who was the club president, was waiting. We were getting out of the airplane, and he said, "Well, that was pretty good."

"Yeah, we kind of had to drop the bags in a hurry. I just wanted to go for a ride."

"What are you talking about? You won the contest. There was one bomb just outside the white rim and the other two were right in the middle of it."

FLYING HAS STUCK WITH ME my whole life. It didn't turn out to be my career the way I thought it would, but it's always been inside me. And over the years, I've had some great experiences in the air.

One of my favourites was getting a chance to fly with the Snowbirds, the famous Canadian Forces aerobatics team.

One summer, I heard that they were coming to St. John's for an airshow. I knew that they were going to be flying in Toronto just before that, so I phoned the base in St. John's to find out where they might be staying. They were at the Skyline Hotel, right out by the Toronto airport. I called the morning of the day they were scheduled to fly into St. John's—I knew they would have to be up early to get the aircraft ready.

I got hold of someone on the front desk at the hotel and asked if the Snowbird pilots were still there. It turned out that they were and some of them were in the lobby, wearing their red flying suits.

They called one of the pilots over and put him on the phone, and it turned out he was the lead guy of the team. I introduced myself and he said he knew me from hockey. I told him that I'd noticed they were going to be doing some flights for the media in St. John's the day before the airshow. I said, "Look, I've got to be on one of those." "No problem," he said. "We'll have you penned in for a flight tomorrow."

I did what I was supposed to do—go to the airport and meet them and get a medical. Then we had a good two-hour briefing about what to expect during the flight and what to do if there was an emergency and you had to bail out—you had to learn how to use the ejector seat. For a flying nut like me, even that was a great experience.

Then it was time to go. The guy I flew with was piloting the number-four aircraft in the formation. His position was tucked right under the tail of the lead, with two more planes off his wingtips. There were nine in formation altogether.

After about ten minutes of flight time we all broke off and were on our own. The pilot started talking to me in my headset.

"I understand you did some flying. You want to fly, don't you?"

Yes, I did. And so he gave me control of the plane. That was amazing.

Then I asked him about aerobatics. Can I do a roll? I'd never done a roll before. I'd done a spin and loops and stuff like that in lighter aircraft, but you couldn't get them to roll. He said I could do it—he'd do a roll first, and then he'd let me do one. So he did one—a full 360 degrees—and then told me I had control again.

I did my roll and I thought it was pretty good, but I lost a few feet of altitude.

"Can I try another one?" I asked him.

The next time I got the stick a little further back and used a bit more pressure. That one was fine—the horizon stayed where it should, a full roll. It was gorgeous.

I ran into the Snowbirds a couple of times after that. One year I was in Halifax for Danny Gallivan's golf tournament. The Snowbirds were in town, and they asked me to do the announcing for their show—which I did. I was supposed to fly with them, too, but the doctor who did my medical didn't want to pass me.

They came to St. John's two years later, and I did the announcing again. And that time, I got up with them—again, in the number-four plane.

The pilot let me take the controls and said, "Bob, you're flying her pretty good. Do you feel like landing the airplane?"

Are you kidding? I'd love to.

He set her up and I landed her on runway 29 at the St. John's airport. It came down nicely. The pilot was cheering. He was delighted. It was a great thrill for me.

After the show, the Snowbird pilots all got me to sign their log books.

They are the best. Some people talk about the Blue Angels, the American aerobatics team, but the Canadian guys taught them how to do some of their manoeuvres. Our guys are tops. I'll never forget those two rides with them.

A FEW YEARS AGO, I took one last turn as a pilot. My son, Robbie, has his private licence, and he's also a commercial helicopter pilot.

I was visiting him out in British Columbia and one day we rented an airplane just outside Vancouver. A funny thing happened. I hadn't had my hands on an airplane for what must have been thirty years. I took the wheel and it felt great. We were flying around and did a few turns. And I turned to Robbie and said in the headset, "I'm going to land her. Is that okay? You're the captain." He said, "You have control." We lined up for a right-hand turn—which I never did get quite comfortable with, but this one was okay. Went in, landed the airplane, and it just came back to me so nicely. I brought her back to stall speed and put her down as smooth as you could.

Robbie looked at me and said, "Where did you learn to do that?"

I opened the throttle for touch and go and he calmly reached over and rasied the flaps to a take-off setting. We went up again, but I screwed up the second landing. I got shagged up on the approach. I guess I should have quit while I was ahead.

But I love the flying, boy. It's something else.

5

ON THE AIR

I had decided not to go into the air force, though I hadn't entirely given up on my dream of flying yet. But I didn't really know what I wanted to do.

I finished high school in 1951. I wasn't fussy about going to work, so I made an excuse to go back to school and do chemistry, just to get another science in case I went on to university.

The London Theatre Company had just opened and they rented our auditorium at Bishop Feild College. Leslie Yeo was the company's director and lead actor. He had come over from England with his wife, Hilary Vernon, who was also an actor, and started the company in St. John's. That went on for a few years, before he moved on to Stratford and the Shaw Festival.

In Newfoundland, the theatre ran for about fifteen or twenty weeks a year. Monday was rehearsal day. Then shows daily except

Sunday, which was a day off. All great plays. So I decided to get involved with that. Really I was just passing time.

I was an assistant to the stage manager, John Holmes, who was an actor, too. They were all actors from the West End in London. Jeez, they were good. The auditorium only held three or four hundred and the stage wasn't really big enough, but they sold out most shows.

I did a lot of the prompting, working behind the curtain in a corner. "Tabs," they call it. When I'd sense that one of the actors was stalled, I'd speak the line quietly. I got pretty sharp at that stuff, watching the little white light and then the red light for the warnings with the cues.

When they staged *Ten Little Indians*, they gave me a different job. In the first act of the play, a voice comes out of the heavens and accuses the characters of committing the murders. I was the voice. I remember them teaching me how to round it off a bit so that I made a more British sound when I said the word "murder"—"It's *muh-duh*, Bob, *muh-duh*."

I guess that went pretty well, because they wanted me to play a role in their next production, *Wuthering Heights*. But I wouldn't do it because there was a scene where the character I was to play (Heathcliff) had to wear short pants. I knew my classmates would be watching just to see me in short pants. There was no way I was going to let that happen. So I didn't do it and blew my first acting opportunity. But I had a great time with the London Theatre Company. They taught me a lot, by how professional they were.

AFTER FINISHING HIGH SCHOOL, I picked up jobs wherever I could. I worked at a garage in the Hertz car rental outlet, doing everything around the office—payroll and stuff like that. But I didn't like it much. So one day I went down to Crosbie and Co., which ran a number of different businesses in Newfoundland including a small air service that was flying out of St. John's. I figured I might get on there and start flying. They didn't have anything for me right away, but in the interim they offered me a job at the Newfoundland Margarine Company Limited, which was owned by the same family. I was making butter (well, really, margarine, which played a small and strange part in the story of Newfoundland joining Confederation, which you can look up if you like). That didn't lead anywhere, so I moved on. My sister had a pretty good job at Gerald S. Doyle, which was a wholesaler in St. John's. She got me a job there for a while.

I was at everything and anything until that night we went down to VOCM.

It was a fluke, really. In June 1954, a bunch of us were hanging out at the Colonial Store on Military Road, right across from the Colonial Building, which used to be the seat of government in Newfoundland. It was a place where you could have a Coke or a Pepsi and talk about baseball and stuff like that. One of the guys came in—Wilf Dyke, who'd been in our class in high school. He had a job as a radio operator at VOCM. The week before, some of the guys had gone down there and had a bit of fun after the station signed off at one in the morning. Wilf and a couple of his buddies got fooling around with tapes and recording things and listening to their own voices. He said, "Coley, we should try that. We should go down there tonight." Yeah, sure, I'm game. So two or three of us went down innocently enough. The announcers that night, Jim Regan and Harry Brown, signed off, and then we started to have some fun.

That station had a great history. It was the first private broadcaster in Newfoundland. Its first studio was in the house of its founder, Walter Williams. You can tell from the first two call letters—VO—that it dates from before Confederation. Those were the letters assigned to the Dominion of Newfoundland, and only the handful of stations that were on air before 1949 were allowed to keep them. VOCM carried a mix of music, news, and talk. The famous show about Newfoundland history and culture, *The Barrelman*—the one that launched Joey Smallwood's career—had moved over from VONF. And by then, the call letters had become the basis of an advertising slogan. The truth is, they didn't mean anything when the station originally went on the air, but by then everyone believed they stood for The Voice of the Common Man.

It just happened that VOCM was looking for an announcer at the time. There were only four of them, and they were going nuts with overtime and everything else. They were dying to hire another guy. We were fooling around with commercials and stuff and the guys happened to like the sound of my voice. I remember Jim and Harry saying, "Bob, you have to come down and make an audition tape." No kidding? Do you really think so? Getting a radio job? Are you joking? I'd take it for nothing. So they lined it up for me to make the tape.

I heard that they looked at seventy-three other guys for the job. But I got it.

My first radio assignment was reading the news and doing commercial spots and the usual deejay stuff. Two hours in the afternoon usually, or sometimes I'd work from seven in the evening until sign-off at one. At night we did two fifteen-minute newscasts—one local and one national. Most of the programming was pre-recorded shows from away. There was one called *Thesaurus* that included different segments—I remember one with Sammy Kaye and his orchestra—then there'd be fifteen minutes of *The Liberace Show*. I'd do a bit of deejaying in between. Then at eleven o'clock the sports news came on. A different guy came in for that. From quarter after eleven to sign-off I did a regular deejay nighttime show, ad libbing and introducing records by people like Eddie Fisher and my all-time favourite, Frank Sinatra.

After a while, I started doing that eleven-fifteen sports report. I did everything. Baseball. Track and field. Whatever they could sell, I'd do it, because I played baseball and hockey. So I was the guy to do the sports.

After I got into the business, I started to listen to a lot of radio—but in St. John's it wasn't that simple. There was an American air force base in town, and I got to know some of the guys and became a member of their NCO club. I heard a lot of great music there, and one of the fellows on the base helped me get a new Zenith radio. I rigged up an antenna on the roof of our garage so I could pick up just about everything on the low-frequency band. WNEW in New York, with Jack Lazare. And I was picking up hockey games. I was always a late-night listener in my room, and I was enthralled by the radio announcers. I remember practising at the kitchen table after everyone had gone to bed. I'd have the newspaper out pretending I was reading the news. "In New York today . . ." Trying to sound like an announcer.

More and more, I thought about broadcasting hockey. I heard Budd Lynch from Detroit and Fred Cusick from Boston. I picked them all up. But I was after something impossible. I don't know why I even had that crazy thought. There was only one announcer for hockey in Canada—Foster Hewitt. Later, there was also Danny Gallivan. I didn't have the audacity to say that I'm going after that job. But I always said, boy, would I ever love to do that.

Eventually, I decided to do something about it. I figured I'd make my own audition tape. I borrowed a tape recorder and did the play-by-play of a St. John's senior hockey game.

It's hard to explain how big senior hockey was in St. John's in those days, but consider this. Two of the private radio stations in town—VOCM, where I worked, and CJON, the station founded by Geoff Stirling (who later started NTV, the private television "superstation" broadcasting out of St. John's) and Don Jamieson (who wound up serving in Lester Pearson's federal Cabinet)—both broadcast the senior games. That is, the same games, at the same time. Denys Ferry did the broadcasts for us, along with Harry Brown. (Denys was a talented actor, as well, and had been held in a prisoner-of-war camp during the Second World War, so he was kind of a hero of mine. His son, David, is a well-known Canadian stage actor now.) They were in one booth in the old St. John's Memorial Stadium. And across from them, the guys from CJON were broadcasting the same game from another booth.

I took my tape recorder and headed for the stadium. I'd been imitating Foster Hewitt all my life, and now I was going to see if I could do a real hockey game. With the two broadcast booths being used, I got permission from the stadium manager to go up on the catwalk high above the ice. Now picture this. I had to climb up a ladder on the side of the building, get up on the catwalk—which was about three feet wide—and then lie down on my stomach to call the game, because that was the only way I could see the ice. I was down at one end, behind a goal, way up high. I called about ten minutes of the action into that tape recorder and then headed back to the station. Jim McGrath happened to be there that night. Later, he would go on to have a successful career in politics, and ended up being the lieutenant-governor of Newfoundland and Labrador. But in those days he was an advertising salesman at the station. And Jim Regan was there, too. He had come to Newfoundland from Windsor, Nova Scotia, and become an announcer (his brother, Gerald Regan, became the premier of Nova Scotia).

I wanted to play the tape right away to hear what it sounded like, and they listened with me. The two of them got kind of excited. Everybody thought it was okay, and Jeez, I did, too. Jim McGrath wanted a copy of the tape right away. He said, "Can you let me have that? I want to take it down to the Harris & Hiscock department store. They'll buy advertising on hockey. I guarantee that they will." He was pleased with the sound of it. So he did, and they told the station, we want this guy to do the games.

Harold and Joe Butler were the two brothers who ran the station. Remember, they already had Harry Brown doing the broadcasts—he was a great announcer, who went on to do *As It Happens* with Barbara Frum and have a long career at the CBC. They listened to my tape, and now they wanted to find a place for me. Harold said,

"What I think we should do is give you a chance to do the second period of the senior hockey broadcasts. I don't think you can do three periods yet. That would be too much." So I started off doing the second period. But then people started talking, I guess. After the first couple of games, I did the first and third and Harry Brown did the second. Now I'm catching on.

I was still playing hockey in those days, too, for the Feildians. For a few years, Harry Brown would take over for me if I was playing the same night as one of our broadcasts. I made the Capitals—the St. John's all-star team—in 1957. I was only one of three guys on that team who didn't play for the local powerhouse, St. Bon's.

One night the commercial league was playing after the senior league game—those were teams sponsored by local businesses. Two local bakeries in St. John's were playing against each other that night. They wanted to have the game broadcast, so they bought the time—and they wanted me to do it. I did the senior game and then went right into the commercial league game after they cleaned the ice. Two games in one night.

After that, never again did I do just the first and third periods. It was the whole game from then on. I got five dollars a game to start, and then CJON called and they wanted to talk to me—it was getting competitive now. VOCM raised me to ten dollars a game. I was doing four games a week. Are you kidding me? I was the highest-paid announcer there—and the youngest. Jim Regan, Harry Brown, Denys Ferry—these were all class guys. But because I was doing the hockey games I was making more money than all of them. Then CJON called again and I had an interview with Geoff Stirling and Don Jamieson. They had stopped doing games by then, but they wanted to get back into it. There were no radio rights. They would just take me and go. Geoff was really persuasive, trying to get me to take a job over there. "The guys are ready to go and sell it right now if you come with us," he said. And I was going to get fifteen bucks a game.

So that got me a raise at VOCM to fifteen dollars a game. I was taking home sixty dollars a week extra. Driving a nice convertible. Life was pretty good.

IT WAS INTERESTING HOCKEY, and very entertaining. I called some games that were 17–3 and stuff like that, crazy high scoring, and others that were real barn burners. In the third period of our games there would be more people at the stadium than in the first period because the game sounded pretty good on the radio, and people would say, "Jeez, there's a good game going on—I'd better get down there." At least that's what they used to tell me.

I remember one huge game. St. Bon's had won twenty-four Boyle Trophy championships in a row—which was the city's senior hockey championship. When would they ever be beaten? St. Pat's had a pretty good team that year, and as it turned out the game was played on the eve of St. Patrick's Day. That was the night St. Pat's beat St. Bon's and broke the streak. Transistor radios had just come out, and they told me that all the city bus drivers had the game on in their buses that night. And at the big theatre in town, the Paramount Theatre on Harvey Road, they piped in the sound of the game during the third period—nobody minded missing the movie because they wanted to hear if St. Pat's could beat St. Bon's.

The whole city was caught up in it. It was big-time stuff. I still have a tape of the broadcast from that night. The crowd in the stadium sounds like they're at the Forum or Maple Leaf Gardens.

One year I called eighty-one games—that's roughly the equivalent of a full NHL season. I travelled all over the island as far west as Corner Brook.

In March you'd have the playoffs—that's when we'd go on the road and do the big ones. One year Corner Brook won the provincial championship and went on to the Allan Cup, which was being held in Victoriaville, Quebec. I was with CBC by then—I'd left VOCM in 1964 and joined CBC, right before CBC TV came on air in Newfoundland. So they sent me up to Quebec to do the games. My old friend Fleming Mackell was living up there somewhere and they got him to be the colour man. I did Corner Brook versus Victoriaville. Victoriaville were big, tough with a lot of former American Hockey League players. It was murder up there. Our guys didn't see a leg of it. They got beaten, of course. But it was a great experience for me.

THROUGH THOSE EARLY YEARS of broadcasting, I still hadn't completely given up on flying. In 1957, I sold my car and saved up some money from work and decided that I was going to get my commercial pilot's licence. That flying was gnawing at me like you wouldn't believe. I wanted to fly so badly. So off I went to Moncton to get a commercial licence. I got it, and in 1958 I applied to Trans-Canada Airlines. It was pretty hard for a guy with a commercial licence out of a flying club to get hired by an airline. You could do it, but most of the guys had experience from the air force. Thousands of hours. So compared to them I was a rookie. But still I was invited up, went to the ground school in '58, and got ready for the pilot training. Then the big layoff came.

The story was that they had just brought in too many of us. The Vanguard, which had greater speed and capacity than the planes before it, was going to be coming into service soon and then the DC-8 was coming soon after that. They laid off our whole class and the one that came after it. The truth is, I probably wasn't going to make it anyway. They had guys from Europe and everywhere. Most of the pilots were out of the Royal Canadian Air Force. They'd served their six years. They were well experienced—jets and otherwise. They went everywhere—British European Airways, British Airways, Qantas in Australia. Some of them stayed in Canada and eventually got hired on. I met some of them years later when I was flying around for *Hockey Night in Canada* and they'd let me sit in the front of the plane.

People tell you timing is everything. Well, for me, I guess the timing wasn't quite right there. But jeez, I'm still working. If I'd been flying I would have been retired twenty years ago and I'd be sitting in a nice home in Florida.

Instead, I went back home to Newfoundland and back into radio, and began seriously exploring my options.

6

FOR THE LOVE OF
THE GAME

From the time I was a young boy, long before I got into broadcasting, sports were a big part of my life.

Hockey and football—soccer—were my two big sports at Bishop Feild. It was highly competitive. In hockey, our rivals, St. Bon's, had their own rink, so they had the advantage of practice. But we had plenty of ice time, too, on the ponds and lakes. All winter we lived for hockey. Ten-hour games every Saturday. St. Bon's always seemed to win the hockey, but we came close a couple of times. We had a good crowd of athletes in our class. We had a class of forty-something, and in football, eight of the starting eleven came from our year. We won the juniors in 1948 and the seniors in 1949 and 1950. So we had a good swing in football.

There were other sports, as well.

In the summer, we used to go to a place on Quidi Vidi Lake that was set up as a public swimming pool. It had a walkway out into the water and diving boards and a lifeguard. Every fine day in the summer, that's where we'd be. And of course, being down there, we would see the rowing crews practising. It seemed like a natural thing to do someday. The Royal St. John's Regatta was such an important event every summer in the city. I wanted to be a part of that if I could.

For those of you who may not know, the regatta is the oldest annual sporting event in North America. It dates back to at least 1816, and it's pretty certain that there were rowing races on the lake before that. But it's not just the long history that makes it unique. It's the race itself. The six-man—or six-woman—crews race in fixed seat shells, not the sliding seats that you're used to seeing at, say, the Olympics. And when they get to the end of the course, they have to make a turn around a buoy and then row back to where they started. On the men's course, that's a little over a mile and a half. There's nothing else quite like it in the world. If you're from Newfoundland, you'll know about the crew of fishermen from Outer Cove who rowed the famous 9:13 4/5 in 1901—a record that stood until 1981.

And if you're from St. John's, you'll know that regatta day is an official holiday, but even that part isn't like anywhere else. On the morning of the first Wednesday of August, the race committee meets to decide if the weather is suitable (wind is usually the issue). If it is, the regatta is on, no one goes to work, and everyone heads for the lake. If the weather isn't right, the regatta is postponed until the first acceptable day.

I don't think the regatta is as big today as it was when I was young—but then again, we think of all things when we were grow-ing up as somehow better. The crowds are still big. They get fifty thousand people down there. But I think in our day the sport itself was bigger because we knew more of the oarspeople. I remember when Bucky Lewis stroked the Summers crew for six straight championships, and when the city police always had a big rowing team, as did the RCMP. And I remember when the Americans from the Pepperrell Air Force Base got involved and won a couple of championships. They trained, I'll tell you. They used to jog over in their uniforms from the base. They were in the gym over there all the time. This was a big deal.

They still broadcast the races live on NTV. I used to do the broadcasts when I was at VOCM, but when I started rowing myself I had to miss two or three of them.

When I was with VOCM I thought, why don't we put a crew together and get a press race going? So we did and CJON radio got a crew, along with the outfit called Guardian Press. I got one of the veteran coxswains, Jack Kenny, a retired Hall of Famer, to work with us. He was retired but since his daughters Lorraine and Mary worked at VOCM he decided he'd take us on and train us. We were all brand new at it. We won the first race. After that, you're hooked. You can't get away from this now. It's a disease. Rowing gets in your blood. It's something else. And it's hard. Just over a mile and a half from the stakes to the buoys and back. That's over ten minutes of rowing. It's tough.

My sisters Olive and Louise rowed, as well. They both worked at Bowring Brothers department store, which was huge in St. John's, and they got a crew together for Bowring when they brought back the ladies' race—it had been gone for many years at that point. The Bowring Brothers Ladies Crew won the first official woman's race in 1949 and were inducted into the Royal St. John's Regatta Hall of Fame in July 2012. My sister Louise, who was on that crew, spearheaded the return of women to the regatta, and my sister Olive was the stroke. Today, eighty percent of the crews are women, and they love it. Good for them. Early in the morning they're all down there practising and getting ready. They've developed some pretty good oarspeople, too.

I rowed about four or five years before giving that part up. But I was so hooked that I began taking crews out for practice spins as a coxswain. (The cox is the fellow who steers the boat and keeps the crew in rhythm, measuring out the strokes and keeping track of where you are in a race. Between races, you're the one who trains the crew.) I was part of the committee and spent a lot of time down around the boathouse. Whenever anybody came down and their coxswain wasn't there, they'd say, how about helping us out, Bob? And I would. It was great. I loved it.

One year, a group of guys from the university came out and they looked pretty good. They didn't win their race that particular year, but they asked me if I'd be interested in taking them on and becoming their coxswain.

As the cox, you're training the crew as best you can and learning to turn the boat efficiently in a race. You're responsible for the tiller, but I always said that the crew is responsible, too. When the bow side catches the water to help turn her, the stroke side keeps rowing. That boat is sixty feet long—it's a big turn to make in a vessel like that. So when she tips, she'll go to the bow side. If you're not careful, your rowers will get buried on the stroke side. The number-two oarsman is usually the one who moves in the boat and tries to keep her as straight as possible in the turn. It's only a few seconds but it's important.

The other part of the cox's job is encouraging the crew in the race. Everybody is dying out there. I remember when I was rowing, in the first minute I was thinking, what am I doing out here, this is killing me. You know how hard it is. But you somehow have to get it across to them that they're looking great, that this is terrific. You encourage them. And you keep the stroke count. The teamwork in rowing is more important than people think. Those oars have to hit at the same split second. If the stroke is changed from thirty-eight a minute to thirty-six a minute, that's got to happen smoothly. There's a lot of stuff that goes into it, really.

The next year we won our races. Made it to the championship and won that. That was pretty good—it was the best time in about fourteen years.

I got so interested in rowing that when I was in Boston doing NHL broadcasts, I went over to Harvard University and met the rowing coach and we got talking. I got in the boat—they have a moving-water pool where they practise. We talked about the fixed seat as opposed to the sliding seat. I found out a lot of things about rowing that we didn't know back home—nobody talked about them, anyway. New little twists and turns. Then in Toronto I went to the rowing club and chatted with the guys down there. I met this coach from Romania, and we got talking about coxswains and stuff. He was surprised when I told him that I was a coxswain. He said, "You're too big. I'll tell you what, Bob. You show me ten pounds' difference I'll show you three seconds." So I immediately started to lose weight. No beer and cut back on this and that. I lost a few pounds, and it helped. The guy was right—ten pounds really is three seconds. We used to figure that a boat length was three seconds, so that's quite important. I got involved in that stuff and learned and I think it helped our crew. I look at the coxswains now—some of them are so heavy. Guys, you shouldn't do that. But you mind your own business.

The other thing I learned from rowing was how to look after my voice. I was working at the CBC at the time, and I remember the day after the regatta I couldn't speak. I couldn't go in to work. With the excitement of the race and the adrenaline, it's crazy how loud you yell. It really is. But if you're in the business, you can't lose your voice.

So I had a special megaphone built. It came from the guts of a welder's helmet. I had one of the guys in the carpentry shop at the CBC put it together for me. You put it on your head and pulled it down with two little hinges, and it went across the lips. They could hear me through the whole boat right down to the bow. Some guys made jokes about it, but it was perfect—it made sense to me. I think some of the guys are still using them.

Right now I'd probably still go out and help a crew get going if they asked me, but I wouldn't steer. I'd find a smaller guy, someone lighter for that.

I guess I passed the rowing gene on to my son, Robbie, who ended up stroking the eights at Ridley College. When he was about twelve years old, he told me that a group of his buddies wanted to enter a crew in the regatta. You do? You want to go in the regatta? Have any of you rowed before? Nope. The stroke oar they had, his dad knew a bit about it and became the coxswain. But I took them out a couple of times, too, and they won the midget race. That got him hooked.

Then he went to Ridley College in Ontario and he called me one evening and said, "I made the hockey team, but I'm afraid I've told the coach I can't do it because I want to go with the rowing team and you can't do both." Ridley is big in rowing. We talked about it and I hung up the phone and thought, he thinks I'm upset because he's given up the hockey. I called him back and said, "Robbie, you made my day when you told me that you were going to concentrate on rowing and had to quit hockey." And that was the truth. The rowing coach put him on the stroke oar, and I went down several times to watch him practise and compete there.

I ALSO LOVED TO CURL and had a bit of success at it. I skipped the Newfoundland rink in the 1971 Brier in Quebec City, and then again four years later in Fredericton. I represented the province in the Canadian mixed championships in 1965 and 1973, as well. But here's a funny connection for you—curling and Toe Blake, the legendary coach of the Montreal Canadiens.

Toe was a difficult man to get to know. He was very stern. He was obviously a heck of a coach—eleven Stanley Cups in thirteen years. And he had his own little idiosyncrasies.

When I would do a Montreal game on Sunday night radio for CBC, I'd go into town Saturday if they were playing at home. I'd watch the game, and then fly with the Canadiens to New York or Boston or wherever they were going to be playing on Sunday. I'd sit in the spare broadcast booth in the old Montreal Forum. Danny Gallivan was down to my right and René Lecavalier, the great French broadcaster, was to the right of him. Toe and I always sat in that same extra booth. He was retired as a coach by then and was a vice president of the Canadiens.

Toe would usually arrive with maybe two or three minutes gone in the first period, always with that fedora on. He might have had a couple of nips in the lounge before he came in. He sat down beside me, and of course I didn't say a word because you didn't speak to Toe unless he was ready. But after a while we got kind of friendly and I knew how to handle the situation. I wasn't going to bother the guy with stupid comments. He was the greatest coach of all time. I wouldn't say a word about the game or anything. I was a radio broadcaster of hockey, but this was Toe Blake. And, I remember, he always had that hat on.

In the Forum, the out-of-town scores were shown on a board at one end of the building, down to my left. It was tough to see from where we sat. One night, the Rangers were playing in Boston, and we were going to New York on Sunday, where the Canadiens would be playing the Rangers. Toe looked over and asked me, "Is that game in Boston over?"

I couldn't see the scoreboard, but being clever, I thought, I would look at my watch for the time. The game in Boston had started a half hour before the one we were watching in Montreal. Toe Blake asked me a question, and I had to have an answer. I was getting in with this guy.

So I said, "Yeah, Toe, I think it is."

There was silence for about fifteen seconds. And then he slammed his fist down on the counter in front of us. His right-hand fist was huge. Papers flew everywhere. And Toe said, "You *think* it's over? I asked you a question, Bob, and you said, I think it's over? I can think for myself. I want to *know*." And he slammed his fist again. Scared the heavens out of me. I didn't say a word.

Then he reached over and tapped me on the knee and said, "Bob, I just taught you something you'll never, ever forget. When somebody asks you a question and you say, yes, you think it is—I don't want that. I wouldn't ask you a question if all I've got to do is think. I want to know."

So that was a pretty good lesson. I used that line at Memorial University in my speech to the students who were graduating when I got an honorary degree. "Always remember that when somebody asks you something, in whatever business you get yourself into, and you don't know the answer, say, I don't know, but I'll find out." And they all liked it. John Crosbie was the chancellor who conferred the degrees that day, and he said in his speech after, "Bob, I wish you'd told me that years ago."

So the curling. I had been curling for a few years now at home. I'd been to a national mixed championship in 1965 as a second stone with a guy from Saskatchewan—Dave Pedley was his name. We went to Toronto and won four games and lost six. Pretty good. Not great, but pretty good. Then I skipped some games and put a team together and eventually, twice, I got to the Brier.

One Saturday night at the game in Montreal, I was sitting with Toe and we had a break in the action. He said to me, "You know what I've been trying lately? I've gone down to the Montreal Curling Club. Somebody invited me down there and I tried it out. And I'm telling you, that's a pretty interesting game. It's not as easy as it looks." I didn't say anything about my own curling. I just said, "So you like it then?"

Now I'm having a great conversation with Toe Blake. Super. We're talking away. I said, "How do you find the game, Toe?"

"Well, boy, what do you know about the game?"

I said, "I'm okay—I know a bit about it."

"I'm playing lead," he said. "There's four on the team, and I'm playing lead."

Yeah, I know that's how it works.

"The worst thing I find is the out-turn. I can throw an in-turn better than I can an out-turn."

"You know what you should do?" I said. "You should go down to the club and go out on the ice by yourself and throw out-turn after out-turn after out-turn." I told him that because that's what I used to do. We all did it.

"What are you, an expert all of a sudden?" Toe said. He was kind of indignant.

"No, that's just what I do at practice to get used to the out-turn. You'd probably get better if you tried it."

Two Saturdays later, we were in the same booth watching a game, and curling came up again. Toe had been promoted to a second stone. He'd moved up. And he was really into it.

So this was in 1971. And in 1971 I went to the Brier in Quebec City as the skip from Newfoundland. And now that Toe was curling, he'd started watching it on TV. And he saw his buddy who'd been sitting next to him in the booth on Saturday night.

Well, the next time I came up to Montreal he pounded that big fist again.

"You must have had some fun with me. You didn't tell me you curled. How come you didn't tell me?"

He was pretty cheesed off, but it was fun.

After that he invited me to his bar on St. Catherine Street. He said, "On your way back to your hotel after the morning skate, drop in." I did and he called me into the back office. It was a mess. Files all over the place. He opened a big drawer and out came a bottle of Scotch. I didn't drink Scotch but I had to have a drink with Toe Blake. He poured and we talked hockey.

I got along famously with him after that.

I LOVE DOGS. Growing up I always had a puppy. Lo and behold they'd get lost, they'd get stolen, they'd get hit by a car. I was broken-hearted so many times. But dad, working at the prison camp, always had access to a new litter, so I wasn't without a puppy for very long. I grew up all the way through with a dog. They were part of our home.

But it wasn't until years later, as an adult, that I discovered one of the real loves of my life: golden retrievers. Let me tell you the story.

In the summer of 1967, Byng Whitteker came out to Newfoundland. He had been a big wheel announcer with the CBC for years, covering things like royal visits. On air, he was very proper, and he had a beautiful deep voice.

This was the year of Expo '67, the world's fair in Montreal. A lot of the CBC's top announcers—people like Lloyd Robertson—had been called in to work there. Byng's job was to find some replace-ments for the summer. He talked to all twelve of our announcers and I was one of the guys chosen to go to Toronto for the summer.

Karen and I had only been married for a year. We rented a place north of the city for the summer. It was lonely for her, but I was working hard. We did the full schedule of everything that announcers did in Toronto—classical music and news and whatever else was on the program. We worked long hours.

On Wednesdays we would get together with Byng and John Rae at a hotel on Jarvis Street near the old CBC headquarters to go over our work. John was one of the top commercial readers in the country, and in those days he got all of the advertising contracts from New York—stuff like "Scope, first thing in the morning and your breath feels fresher all day…" Absolutely terrific voice. John would give us announcing tips and Byng would talk to us about how to handle different kinds of events. We became great friends with Byng. He would invite us over to his apartment for dinner.

One weekend Karen and I had a car and went on a drive north of Toronto. We wound up in an area near Markham where there seemed to be a lot of dog kennels. We decided to stop at this one place, Forget Me Not Kennels. There was a lovely area of green grass. Dogs were running around and playing. And this gorgeous golden-looking dog came over to the fence where I was looking and jumped up and put her paws towards me. Bingo.

I knew a little bit about golden retrievers. Paul Johnson, a very successful insurance man in St. John's, had one, which in those days may have been the only one in Newfoundland. This golden that jumped up, her name was Candy and it looked like she was close to having pups. So I went in to the building and met the owners and I said I've got to have one of those pups. They were fine with that, but they made me promise to show the dog in professional dog shows. Now I'd never done that, but I promised, and it was done. The puppy was weaned at eight weeks and they sent him down to me just before Christmas in '67. We called him Byng—like Byng Whitteker. That was our first golden.

Christian was just born, and Hilary was born after that, and Byng immediately was their guardian. He'd lie down by Christian's door every day. When the baby was in sleeping, Byng would find a place there and he wouldn't move.

So we decided we had better get another one. A guy named Jim Osborne, who lived out in Conception Bay near where we were living, had a female golden that he had brought over from England. So the puppies were born and Byng was a father and I got the pick of the litter. We called him Bogey.

As I mentioned, I didn't know anything about showing dogs, but I had to keep that promise. I took Byng to the Newfoundland Kennel Club show in Harbour Grace. We stayed with George Faulkner there, from the hockey-playing Faulkner family. I showed Byng twice and he got his championship. I didn't know a thing. I should have had a handler do it. But that's how good the dog was. He was the champion and I had absolutely nothing to do with it.

And I'll bet you he was the only golden retriever that ever drank out of the brier championship trophy. Jack McDuff skipped the Newfoundland rink to the title in 1976—the only rink from the province that's ever won. He brought the trophy up to our house and we got a picture of Byng sipping champagne out of the tankard. So thank you Jack McDuff!

When Byng had to be put down, we were all shaken by that. Twelve years of togetherness. By then there were golden retriever kennels popping up all over the place in Newfoundland. So we got our third, Figaro, and he was followed by Davern, and finally Woody, who we lost ten or eleven years ago.

All of them were like part of the family.

IF I'M TALKING about other sports I love, I should probably mention Atlantic salmon fishing. One of my favourite things is to be on a river with a fly rod in hand, and my home province, Newfoundland and Labrador, has some of the best salmon-fishing waters in the world. Salmon aren't easy to catch—that's why they're sometimes called the fish of a thousand casts—and the only way you can catch them legally is with a fly, but it's worth the effort and the challenge when one of them takes the fly, leaps into the air, and then strips hundreds of feet of line off your reel. Like a lot of my fellow Newfoundlanders, I've made it one of my summer passions.

As a boy, when my father was running the prison camp out on the Salmonier Line, he used to get me to bring government visitors from St. John's to the salmon pools on the Salmonier River. I'd show them how to get in. I might get a quarter or fifty cents— pretty good money back then. That's how I started my salmon-fishing career. I hooked my first fish there and landed it. A warden told me it was the biggest he'd seen in years—a little over twelve pounds. That was a big fish for the Salmonier, which is usually a grilse river (grilse are the small salmon that come back into the river after only one winter in the ocean).

It was a hell of a day.

But I didn't really get into salmon fishing as an adult until a chance encounter while I was working at VOCM. Non-anglers might not recognize the name, but for anyone who has an interest in fly-fishing, there was no one more famous than Lee Wulff. He was an American, a master fisherman and fly tyer, a pilot and explorer, a guide and filmmaker and entrepreneur. Wulff came to Newfoundland after the war and started bringing Americans up to fish in the rivers on the west coast and in Labrador. He made a bunch of films about salmon and trout fishing in Newfoundland. At one point, he tried to convince Joey Smallwood to let him manage the sports fishery for the entire province, but that didn't happen, and eventually he moved on. He's been dead for almost thirty years now, but you can still find some of the flies he designed in any fishing store.

And I got to meet him in person.

It was when I was working at the station in the early days, dee-jaying and reading the news, playing records—just normal radio station stuff. One Sunday evening I was alone in the station and went to the teletype to get some news for ten o'clock. On my way there, I met this gentleman who'd walked up the three flights of stairs to the VOCM offices.

I said, "Sir, can I help you?" He said, "I was just out for a walk and I heard the music coming out of that window on McBride's Hill. I thought I'd drop in and say hello." So I said, "Sure, c'mon in. Nothing going on." He sat down in the waiting area and I went out to the teletype and got the news, and then I said, "Why don't you come on in the booth and sit down here so we can chat.

"What brings you to St. John's?"

"Well, I've got my own airplane down at Quidi Vidi Lake. I've got her docked down there, a Super Cub."

"Oh, a Super Cub. I just learned to fly last summer on a Cub J-3 in Yarmouth. Well, we've got something in common."

"I didn't get your name, sir."

"I'm Bob Cole."

"Hi, Bob. I'm Lee Wulff."

Of course I just about passed out. I'd been reading about salmon fishing and Lee Wulff and here he was with his own airplane—he'd been filming, that's what he'd been doing. So the conversation went on and on.

He invited me to come up to Labrador with him—he was doing some filming for Joey Smallwood. (The weight was too much with an extra man, so in the end it didn't happen.)

We got talking about salmon fishing. I had read that he was the greatest salmon fisherman in the world. I believed it. He told me stories about how to fly-fish for salmon, what to do with the flies you were casting, what kind of fly, what size of fly. Different conditions. He just blinded me with all the facts.

And I said, "Tell me, Mr. Wulff—"

"Call me Lee," he said.

"—let's say I go salmon fishing. I've been to the rivers. I've taken people in and shown them where the pools were when I was a little boy. But I've never really fished much for salmon. Never really fly-fished."

"Okay," he said, "we'll start from scratch." And he did. Casting. Watching for movement in the water. How to wait, how to go back at them, how the presentation of the fly is so important.

"And if you ever hook a salmon," he told me, "the first thing you do is get your rod up immediately, get a tight line, make sure the hook is set, and then let the salmon dictate what's going to happen. The salmon is the boss. Not you. Whatever she wants to do, that's what happens. You play that salmon until it's ready to be reeled in. Sometimes it takes ten minutes and sometimes it takes an hour. There's a lot of fun in salmon fishing. You'll be fine."

We went fishing the next week and, lo and behold, I hooked a salmon. And I've got to say, thank you, Lee Wulff.

I've been salmon fishing ever since.

NEWFOUNDLAND MAY HAVE the best salmon fishing in the world, but for most Newfoundlanders, fishing is serious business. Well, for a few years I tried my hand at the business side of things myself.

Capelin are small fish that look a bit like smelt or sardines. Every spring, they gather in huge numbers to spawn off the shores of Newfoundland. They roll up on the beaches where people collect them in buckets. But until the Japanese came along in the 1980s, there really wasn't much of a commercial fishery for them. In Japan, the female capelin, full of eggs, are considered a delicacy. I had met a fellow named Karl Sullivan through the Newfoundland government and Karl and I thought we'd try to get in on that business.

We looked around and found a place down in Pouch Cove, about fifteen minutes outside of St. John's, an old snack bar and restaurant that had closed down. We brought in contractors and fixed it up and made it look like a fish plant is supposed to with the freezing and the cold storage. And I met this Japanese buyer,

Nuboro Ishiwata. We called him "Ishy." Ishy and I became fast friends and he helped me get set up.

The capelin fishery takes place over a three or four-week period in the late spring and early summer, and it's all very confusing. I didn't know much about the fish business so I decided I'd go over to the fisheries college and took some courses and tried to learn as much as I could. Then we needed to go out and find a fisherman, and we did, Alex Day. He had his own long-liner set up for the capelin fishery. We became buddies and he agreed to deliver capelin to our plant.

Now you needed a trucker lined up and "reefers"—a refrigeration unit—organized and a staff and you have to teach them something that you just learned. But somehow we got it all going. And just as we did, Karl my partner was offered a job in France. So I was left alone— and brother, did I need help. I got a lot of it from Ishy and Alex Day and other fishermen who came along and supplied the plant.

When the hockey season was over I was right into it. I spent all of my time at the fish plant. I event slept down there. I rigged myself up with a nice little cot and everything. Shea Foods was the name of the business. It lasted for about eight years, and every year I was learning something new. We moved along pretty well until the fishery itself became a problem. The fish got smaller because of a change in the water temperature, and the market in Japan started to shrink. We had thirty or forty workers employed when we were up and running and we processed other stuff as well—squid for the bait fishery, and mackerel and a bit of cod, but capelin was our bread and butter. Everything got to be pretty difficult. You had to be really careful to make a go of it.

Finally, a guy came along in 1988 and was looking to buy. I said I'm getting out and it saved my neck a little bit. But it was a great experience. I met a lot of great people. Those long-liner fishermen, they're hard working.

But now, thinking back, my favourite part of the experience was an innovation I came up with—one that involved my kids.

Remember these were the days before cell phones were in common use. When the capelin begin arriving, they start on the west coast of Newfoundland, then St. Mary's Bay, around the Avalon Peninsula, Conception Bay, Trinity Bay, Bonavista Bay, Notre Dame Bay, White Bay and on up the Northern Peninsula.

The trick was to try and keep in touch with the boats so you knew when they were coming in with a load of fish and be ready to meet them at the dock with a truck to take the fish to the plant. And you'd better be there before someone else comes along and scoops up that load for themselves.

I decided the best way to do that was to set up a VHF radio so that I could be in direct contact with the captains on the water. I set one up in my car, and another one at my home in Topsail. The call letters were VCG—Victor Charlie George—307.

When I was at the plant or out in the car I had my daughters Hilary and Megan listening to the radio, which I had set up in the rec room. Whenever they heard "VCG 307," they were supposed to get to it as soon as possible. I guess I broke a few rules there, but I schooled them pretty good. Remember, these were seven- and eight-year-old girls we're talking about. The captains couldn't believe it.

"VCG here," they'd answer.

"We're trying to get in touch with Bob."

"We'll have him call you right away, sir."

Then I started to give them all the lingo to use, so they could communicate with the guys on the boats. The language can get a little dicey out there—all of the captains listen to the same channel so they know where the other boats are and what they are doing. But when they called the girls, I'd get them to move up to another frequency so they could talk in private. Imagine those conversations.

"What's your load? Over"

"Looks like we've got 40,000."

"Stand by. I'll have Bob call you right away. Don't worry. The truck will be there."

The guys got a huge kick out of it. "You should hear Bob Cole's girls," they'd say. "They're better than he is on the radio."

LET ME TELL YOU one more fishing story. The late Craig Dobbin, the Newfoundland businessman who founded Canadian Helicopters—which became the biggest helicopter company in the world—was a great friend of mine. He bought a salmon-fishing lodge in Labrador, and he invited me up there to fish along with the former premier of Newfoundland Frank Moores.

I'm fishing away there on a nice pool and having a pleasant day. Along comes a canoe down through the rapids and into the smooth part, down by me. Two Aboriginal fellows in the canoe went on by. That was all. Nothing more to it than that. Down to the mouth of the river.

A couple of days later I was sitting around the lodge with Craig, his wife, and two or three other friends, having a chat and maybe a beer or something. A knock came on the screen door behind me. I got up and said, "Jeez, there's the same two fellows at the door."

Now, George Bush—the first President Bush—had become friends with Craig, and he'd just been up there. He'd caught his first salmon.

President Bush had just left last week. Now these two guys were at the door. I said, "Do you want to see Craig Dobbin?"

"No," one of them said. "We want to see you. Bob Cole. *Hockey Night in Canada.*"

Good God. Here I am in the middle of nowhere and they want to see me. Craig said, "I had the president of the United States up here all last week and no one noticed, but now you're here and they want to see you."

The point I'm making is that *Hockey Night in Canada* is just so big. Bigger than me. Bigger than any other television show. That's why they came back over that big stretch of water in their canoe to see me.

We got some pictures taken and I signed some autographs. It was a great little visit.

7

A HELL OF A TRIP

It was the summer of 1956. I was working for VOCM. I had a few dollars saved up, and I had an idea—a road trip to New York City. There was Hank Mews, who was a great centre-half in football. His father was the mayor of St. John's, one of the finest mayors we ever had. And there was Hubert Bourne, who'd been in my class in school. His father owned a service station on Torbay Road where we'd go to get an oil change or new tires. Anything to do with cars, Hubert would look after us. I said to them, "Why don't we go to Toronto first. We'll buy a car there—Hubert can give us a hand picking it out because he knows cars. Then we'll take off for a two-week holiday and head for New York."

The truth is, we didn't know what we were doing. We went out to Toronto first and drove down Yonge Street—we'd heard that was the place to go. There were all kinds of car lots there. And we came up with this '54 Meteor—so only two years old. We bought it and hit the road for New York City. It was the first time I'd been there since I had worked on the ship as a bell boy.

The first thing I did when we got there was talk my way into the game at Yankee Stadium. I told them I was a sports broadcaster from Newfoundland, that I worked for a station called VOCM, and as amazing as it seems, they let us in. We got into the stadium and looked over from where we were sitting and I saw that it was Mel Allen broadcasting. Now, Jeez. He's our hero. We grew up listening to radio. We didn't have TV yet. Radio was magic. And Mel Allen was the voice of the Yankees—so he was the voice of baseball.

After the game I went down to where Mel Allen was and introduced myself. This was nuts. And he was fabulous. Hearing that voice—"Hi, y'all." So I told him everything about me, told him I was a sportscaster back home. He said, "I'm going to do something for you. I'm going to give Bob Fishel a call." Bob Fishel was the public relations guy for the Yankees, and on Allen's say-so he got us three tickets for the next night's game. I think it was Cleveland that was in town and it was Billy Martin's first game with the Indians. Fishel also got me, Bob Cole, a pass to the dugout and the field before the game. Jeez.

We got there an hour before batting practice. The boys took their seats and I marched down to the dugout and waited for the players to come out of the tunnel. I was sitting in the Yankees dugout all by myself, and Gil McDougald came out—he was the first one. I told him where I was from, and now the other players were arriving. They'd been in the batting cage hitting balls into the seats. Gil said to me, "Have you met any of the guys?" I said, "No, you're the first one." "Well, come out with me." I walked out on the field with my Brownie camera. I didn't know anything about taking pictures. I walked out with Gil McDougald and he called Mickey Mantle out of the batting cage. Mantle came out of the cage to talk to me. I had enough class not to ask Gil to take a picture of me with Mickey. I wouldn't do that. That would be terrible. But I asked Mickey if I could take his picture.

It was a night game, but it was still so bright in the stadium under the lights. I set up to take the picture and Mickey said to me, "I don't know if that's going to come out very well. Do you have a flash on that thing?" I said, "Jeez, I think so." He said, "Well, you'd better take another one." This is Mickey Mantle, 1956. The year he won the Triple Crown, .353, 130 RBI, and 52 homers. I put the flash on and took the picture. I've still got the two pictures at home.

So here I was taking a picture of Mickey Mantle holding a bat on the field in Yankee Stadium. I looked up in the seats and spotted Hank and Hubert watching me—they had to be thinking, what is he up to now? I went back to the dugout, talked to the guys for a while, and then politely said thank you and left. Went up to my seat.

That night after we got back from the baseball game, I said, "Boys, if we're in New York we've got to see a Broadway show while we're here." They had never been to anything like that and neither had I, but I knew a bit about what was going on because of my deejay work at the radio station. *Mr. Wonderful* was the big show then, with Sammy Davis Jr. and the Will Mastin Trio. We got three tickets and it was great. After the show I said, "Listen, let's find the door to backstage." We went around the building and found it. Sure enough, Jack Carter, the comedian in the show, and Sammy Davis Jr. came out. We met Sammy and had a chat. Short guy. What a talent.

I'm always doing stuff like that. It was a hell of a trip.

AFTER THE TIME IN NEW YORK, we drove back to Toronto. And that's when I started to think about the tape in the back of the car—the play-by-play audition tape I made up on the catwalk of Memorial Stadium in St. John's. I'd thrown it in my bag with half a thought that I might pass it along to someone.

We were driving back through the city, and I didn't really know where we were. I said, "Guys, we're going through Toronto. I'm going to find Foster Hewitt's radio station." So I headed downtown and found my way around Yonge Street and we passed this street and that. I think it was Grenville Street where Foster's station, CKFH, was located. I parked the car around the corner on Yonge and said to the guys, "I'm just going to drop off this tape. I'll be right back." So I left them there sitting in the '54 Meteor.

I walked into the station and asked the receptionist if Mr. Hewitt was in. She said, "Yes, do you have an appointment?" "No, no, I'd just like to leave this tape and ask him if he'd listen to it." She said just a minute and she called him on the phone, and then she said, "Come with me, Mr. Cole." Jeez, she brought me into his office. There was a big oak chair and desk, and cripes, there was Foster Hewitt sitting there. This was nuts. I can't even explain how it felt. I grew up listening to this man doing the hockey games and imitating him all my life, and now here I was. I didn't think in a million years that he'd actually see me.

He said, "Bob, what can I do for you?" I just about passed out hearing that voice. I said, "Well, sir, I have this tape here. I do hockey games back home in Newfoundland for our station. I thought if you got a chance to listen to it you could maybe write to me and tell me if I should look for another job or maybe you could give me some help." He said, "Why don't we listen to it now?" That's what he said. "Come with me." We went out to a little spare room with all the tape machines, and an engineer was there. "Charlie, put this tape on for me, please," Foster said. And my voice came on all of a sudden and it sounded so bad. And I had thought it was pretty good, those ten minutes of the Guards and St. Bon's playing a senior game at the stadium.

And I thought, Oh my God.

Foster listened to it and said, "Let's go back in the office." We sat and talked there for about an hour about voice inflections, and what to do and when to do it. He told me you need to set your tones and use them in the right spots. He did say nice things to me about my voice—he said, "I like your voice. The voice is right. But you're going to have to learn to use it for hockey. You have to paint pictures." He explained how it was about the little things you say—the Leafs in their white jerseys and the Canadiens in their red. It hits people's minds, and they picture everything without knowing what you're doing. And afterwards they'll tell you how much they enjoyed the game. He said, "Someday you'll be up here and when you do your game, you'll go home afterwards and your people will tell you they enjoyed it immensely. They'll tell you how exciting it was, what a great game it was. And when they say all that and they don't even mention your name, you'll know you've arrived. You've done the job."

I've never forgotten that. He told me to save the big call for a goal or a terrific save. You have to use the different voice levels. For years I'd listen to air checks of my games and listen for that. You know, I still do it. I still go up when I should and don't go up when I shouldn't. And I can follow a guy down the right side and build the excitement all the way. *Gretzky's in his own zone and makes a nice move to get outside the blue line. And he's loose on that right side*—and then you get it going, get it going, and now . . . you've got it. If you can do that, you'll keep the fan flowing with the game. "Flow, that's the word," Foster said. "Feel and flow." I use that now when I talk to guys about broadcasting.

You've got to smell it. You've got to feel the game. I don't want to sound like I'm the only one doing it. Don't get me wrong—I'm not saying that. But I actually feel what's happening during a hockey game. I can feel it in the butterflies in my stomach. There are twenty thousand people in the arena making hockey noise. I'm up here in the booth, and I can see what the players are going to do. I honestly feel it. I sometimes know when something is going to happen before it does. I'm not right all the time, but sometimes, I just know.

Foster was retired when I got the job with *Hockey Night in Canada*. His son, Bill Hewitt, was calling games then, and Foster knew that I was uncomfortable coming in there when Billy was winding up. It was only once in a while at first. I did seven games a year or something. But it was awkward when they scheduled me for a Saturday night game where Billy might have been. It was a funny feeling. I didn't like to be getting somebody's job. I didn't want that.

I got to really know Foster during the 1972 Summit Series. They brought him out of retirement to do the television play-by-play and I was doing the radio. I knew all the players, including the Soviets, and he really didn't, so he used to go running around before the games at the Luzhniki Arena in Moscow saying, "Where's Bob?" You could hear him all over the place. I had the lineup for him and told him how to pronounce the names and all that. He did a helluva job on that series. He might have messed up a couple of the Canadian names but he got all the Soviet ones down. And his call on that final goal is still the best. "Henderson has scored for Canada." What else could you say?

YEARS LATER, for Foster's eightieth birthday there was a big celebration at one of the swanky golf and country clubs in Toronto. I got a note saying that he'd like me to come the day after the Saturday night game. Instead of getting on the plane home to St. John's, I got a cab and went to Foster Hewitt's birthday luncheon. Anybody who was anybody in Toronto was there. It was packed. The heavyweights. The newspaper owner John Bassett and all that crowd. When I walked in Foster was there with his wife, and when I walked up to him to say happy birthday and thanks for the invite he put his arms around me and whispered in my ear, "Everything is going to be fine." And then later on somebody came up to me and said, "Mr. Hewitt would like you to come over and have your picture taken with him." Jeez. So I went over and we got a picture. That's the way he was. He was a great man.

8

GETTING THE
HANG OF IT

Alex Faulkner, the first Newfoundlander to play in the
National Hockey League, was a friend of mine. He had
come out of Bishop's Falls and played senior hockey in St. John's.
King Clancy of the Toronto Maple Leafs was in St. John's on a visit
and saw Alex play. The Leafs signed him, but he ended up with
the Rochester Americans where he led the AHL team in scoring.

Toronto left him unprotected and in 1960 he was picked up by
the Detroit Red Wings. That's where he finally got a chance to play
in the NHL. Detroit's third line was Alex at centre, Larry Jeffrey on
left wing, Bruce MacGreegor on right wing.

Before he left Newfoundland, he would stay at my place and
I'd stay at his, and we'd joke: "Who's going to make it to the NHL
first, you or me?"

"I think you are," Alex said.

But he beat me by nine years.

I went up to see him with the Red Wings in the spring of 1963 when he had a fantastic playoff, scoring five goals in eight games. Alex introduced me to Sid Abel, who was the Red Wings coach in those days. Sid knew I was an aspiring broadcaster, and he set me up with the PR people in Detroit to let me use one of their booths and record an audition tape. I taped myself calling a game between Montreal and Detroit—a game with names like Gordie Howe and Alex Delvecchio and Normie Ullman and Terry Sawchuk. So now I had an NHL audition tape. Sid liked it. He heard the tape and said, "We'll keep our eyes open for you." But Budd Lynch was doing their broadcasts then and he wasn't going anywhere.

Not a lot of people know this, but I also did a bit of scouting for the Red Wings in Newfoundland. Sid and I were having a drink in a bar one night and I asked him about scouting players— what did he see? What did he look for? He told me that if I ever saw a player back home who I thought might have NHL potential, I should give him a call.

Not long after that I saw this young goalie named Doug Grant playing for Corner Brook in the senior league. He was fantastic. So I called Sid. "I'm going to take your word for it, Bob, and we'll bring him up to take a look," Sid said. "Find out his birthdate— that's important. He's right on the cusp of junior eligibility. We'll see what he's like."

So the Red Wings called, and the kid accepted their offer—and then he got cold feet. He wouldn't tear himself away from home and go up there.

Three years later, he finally went, and wound up with St. Louis and had a decent career—even though he lost those three years.

MY BROADCASTING CAREER in Newfoundland was moving along. In 1964 I left VOCM for the CBC, where I worked as a news anchor. CBC TV came on the air in the province in 1965, and for a couple of years they had me doing both radio and television. I did everything on the news side, including covering elections. And a lot of Newfoundlanders remember that I was the quizmaster on *Reach for the Top*. I did that for thirteen or fourteen years.

At the same time, some people in the broadcasting business on the Mainland were starting to pay attention to my hockey play-by-play.

We followed a team, the Corner Brook Royals, to the Allan Cup in Victoriaville, Quebec, and I was told that Sam Pollock, general manager of the Montreal Canadiens, heard my play-by-play, or at least someone who knew him heard it and told him about me. He was kind of interested in the sound of this guy. Something happened there. My name was pushed around a bit. "There's a guy down there in Newfoundland. . . ."

I was on the executive of the Feildian Athletic Association, and every year we had a guest speaker come out for our dinner. I got King Clancy to come down one year, Rocket Richard another year. And Danny Gallivan. I was driving Danny around on the off-day, and we got talking. He knew that I was broadcasting local games. I asked him what I should do to get closer to a job in the National Hockey League.

"Ralph Mellanby is the executive producer of *Hockey Night in Canada*," Danny said. "Give him a call in Toronto and use my name."

So I called him—this was a Friday. I asked the girl on the *Hockey Night in Canada* switchboard if I could I speak to Ralph Mellanby.

"Who's speaking?"

"Bob Cole from St. John's, Newfoundland."

She said he was in a meeting and I was about to say, well, don't get him out of a meeting for me. But before I could she said, "Stand by."

Oh jeez, I don't want to call him out of a meeting. I'm dead before I start. Who the hell is this calling me? He doesn't know me from a hole in the ground.

Then Ralph picked up the phone. I told him I was a hockey announcer in St. John's, that Danny Gallivan had given me his number, and I'd like to come up and do an audition tape. I said, "I've got tapes of local hockey but I'd like to do an NHL-sounding game. I thought maybe I could come up sometime to Montreal and tape a game."

"How about Wednesday?"

"What do you mean—this Wednesday?"

"This Wednesday. There's an open booth in the Montreal Forum. I'll arrange a pass for you. You get your own tape recorder. Give me a copy when you're done."

So off I go. I rented a tape recorder on Crescent Street and got my brother-in-law, Jim Curran, who lived in Montreal at the time, to sit in the booth with me and keep score. I did the game—Detroit and Montreal. Now I had an audition tape. I picked ten minutes out of that and sent it to Ralph.

SOME OTHER THINGS were happening in the league around that time. In 1967, the NHL expanded from six to twelve teams. That meant there were six new play-by-play jobs opening up. I sent off my tape and waited to hear back.

I got close several times. The Oakland Seals offered me the job. They talked to me in Montreal when they unveiled their new uniforms—gold and green. Tim Ryan was handling the broadcasting part of it for them and asked me to come out. He was going to do some of the hockey—I wouldn't be doing it all. And he was going to be the boss. I think that deterred me from going. I got cold feet. I was scared of the situation there. It turns out I made the right decision, given all the troubles they had with that team. (Of course, Tim later went to New York and did very well.)

In Philadelphia, I finished in the top three for the Flyers play-by-play job. In Minnesota they had seventy-three applicants. They told me I was in the top three there, as well.

In the end I didn't get a job anywhere. But at least my name was out there now in the hockey world.

Still, let's face it—I was an announcer from Newfoundland who had never been anywhere and hadn't done anything off the island. I had to prove myself, I guess. I needed someone to give me a chance.

Allan Gilroy was the head of network sports for CBC. He must have heard that audition tape, and for some reason he liked what I did. And he became an integral part of my first game. In the spring of 1968, he called me and hired me to host the fourth and what turned out to be the final game of the Stanley Cup finals between the Montreal Canadiens and St. Louis Blues on CBC Radio. Ted Darling was doing the play-by-play and Fred Sgambati was doing the colour. They were just giving me the opportunity to go on the network, and there really wasn't much to it. At the beginning of the broadcast, I said, "Good evening, everybody, from the Forum in Montreal, the Stanley Cup playoffs. And now, here's Ted Darling." I also did some network cues and the closing.

That's all I did. Nothing else. They just wanted to hear how I would sound and handle myself on the network.

ONE FUNNY LITTLE ASIDE about that game. Gordie Howe was being interviewed between periods. In the old Forum you had to kind of climb around to get into the booth. And when he climbed down for his interview he saw me. Of course, we had met in Detroit when I was down with Alex Faulkner and again when Gordie came out to Newfoundland to fish.

Gordie looked at me and said, "Here we go—we've got the new Danny Gallivan, have we?"

I was a little embarrassed at that because I wasn't even doing the play-by-play—Ted Darling was.

I GUESS I MADE a bit of an impression because in September 1968, I was called to cover the Olympics in Mexico City for CBC Radio. Ted Darling, who was based in Ottawa then, was supposed to go, but then he got the job hosting intermission on the Canadiens broadcasts and had to cancel the Olympic thing. So they got me to replace him.

My main job was to broadcast the field events, which turned out great. I was based at the Estadio Olímpico Universitario. Don Wittman was in the booth next to me doing the TV stuff. Fred Sgambati and I were in the same booth. Fred was doing the track and I was doing the field. I did the javelin, the pole vault. Dick Fosbury doing his "flop" in the high jump. Some of it was being taken live on the network and some of it was recorded.

And I got to call Bob Beamon's famous long jump, which set a world record that stood for almost twenty-three years—one of the greatest athletic accomplishments of the twentieth century. Beamon skipped his second jump—I guess something just wasn't right for him. And I remember calling it, "And now Beamon for his third and final attempt. There he goes. . . ."

The crowd roared. I could see the marker in the long jump pit that said "Olympic Record" and the marker that said "World Record" and he was past the whole works. I don't remember exactly what I said then—I just kind of went with the feeling in the stadium. I don't have the tape anymore. I wish I did.

When there wasn't any competition going on at the track I did a bunch of other stuff. I was learning on the move down there. I was a raw rookie. But I bluffed my way through it. I was doing rapid-fire pistol shooting on radio. How do you like that? And fencing. They used some of the play-by-play from fencing when the Romanian Ion Drîmbă won it and I went nuts just as if it were a hockey game. They used it. I had no idea what I was talking about—foil or épée or whatever the hell it was. But I had to do it. I worked eighteen hours a day and I loved every minute of it.

THERE WAS A PRESS ROOM at the stadium where all the media had their own desk and typewriter. I had my little spot. One day I spotted an older guy sitting all by himself. He didn't seem to be typing anything. After that I saw him every day. This guy, he looked so lonely. He seemed to be lost.

The next time I saw him there weren't too many people around. Something was going on in the stadium, so they were all over there. And we were left alone in this massive newsroom, this guy and me. I went over and introduced myself. I said, "How are you doing? I see you sitting here all alone. Who do you work for?" He said, "ABC." "Oh, I'm sorry I didn't recognize you. I'm Bob Cole, from CBC Radio. I'm covering the field events. I saw you sitting here all by yourself and I thought I'd say hello. Do you want to get a coffee or something?" He said, "No thanks. You're very kind, though."

"And your name?"

"Jesse Owens."

Yep, Jesse Owens.

I didn't know if I should get down on my knee or what, but am I ever glad I went over to say hello. I just froze. I missed the moment of asking him all the stuff I should have asked. I was just thrilled to death to meet the man. He was obviously a figurehead for ABC at the Games. He wasn't doing anything. He was just there. The great Jesse Owens.

I HAD ANOTHER interesting encounter at those Games.

After the decathlon, I was in the press tent and got a chance to talk to the fellow who won the gold medal, American Bill Toomey. He was sitting by himself and I went over and introduced myself. We got chatting. He was a nice guy, and we were soon fast friends. I said to him, "Listen, I'm new at this. I've got this goddamned big tape recorder to carry around, and you know what would be a great idea? The metric mile is tomorrow and Jim Ryun is the big hope for the United States. I've got a field pass and you've got a field pass. We can go down to the grass, I'll tape the run, and you'll comment with me." He thought it was a fine idea.

Before the race I went down and set up the recorder and hooked up the mikes. Working at VOCM, we learned how to do all of that ourselves. No union in those days. Now I had it hooked up and had Bill Toomey with me.

The metric mile was about to start. And Howard Cosell came over and knelt down right next to Bill. I think he was working for ABC television at those Olympics.

The race started, and of course they had to go around the track four times. Ryun passed us for the second time, and when he made the far turn, you could tell that he was struggling.

"Bill, it looked like there was something wrong. He kind of stumbled there. . . ." Bill said he was seeing the same thing, and I figured I was on to something. Ryun was falling back and guys were passing him. I'm excited. This is going to be a great broadcast. (In the end, Ryun came back and ran a decent time—but it wasn't good enough to beat the great Kenyan runner Kip Keino, who won the gold to Ryun's silver.)

And then right next to me, loud enough that you knew it was going into our mikes, I heard that famous voice.

"Ryun's in trouble! I tell you, Ryun's in trouble!"

He was looking right at us. He saw our mikes. Doesn't matter to him. He's Howard Cosell.

"I tell you, Ryun is in trouble!"

I was ticked right off. He was ruining my whole thing with Toomey.

Thanks a lot, Howard.

WHEN I CAME BACK from Mexico City, it was just about time for the National Hockey League season to start. Allan Gilroy must have liked what he heard from me, because I started getting some assignments doing colour on the CBC Radio Sunday night games, which were broadcast nationally across the network. In terms of colour commentary, the truth is, I didn't know what I was doing. I didn't know what was going on and I didn't like doing it. But for the first game they gave me, in Boston, I was working with the best in the world—Foster Hewitt. That was the first time we'd connected since that meeting in Toronto when I dropped off my audition tape. I didn't have to do much. Foster did everything and it was great. He took me out to dinner afterwards and we had a grand chat about it all.

Later in that season, I also did some games with Bob McDevitt, who was another play-by-play guy, and Ted Darling. But I was always the colour man.

Then, in the playoffs in the spring of 1969, something changed.

We were doing the second-round playoff series between the Canadiens and the Boston Bruins. The winner would go on to face one of the expansion teams in the finals, so this was really the series for the Stanley Cup. On CBC Radio we did Sunday night games, plus any potential deciding games. Bob McDevitt was doing the play-by-play, and I was back doing the colour. The Habs had won the first two games of the series at home, Boston the next two. So it was game five, back in Montreal.

Ralph Mellanby was the executive producer of *Hockey Night in Canada*, and at that time radio was part of what he oversaw. The morning of the game there would always be a television meeting in a hotel suite. After the television part was done, working out all their cues and everything, Ralph would get together with the three of us who were doing radio—the producer, Francois Carignan, and Bob McDevitt and me.

They all knew that I was an aspiring play-by-play guy, and they all must have known that I was pretty terrible at doing colour. At that meeting, Ralph said that tonight, there was going to be a change. I would be doing the play-by-play and McDevitt would be doing the colour. Needless to say, I was thrilled. And McDevitt wasn't. He blew a gasket.

I went back to my room at the Mount Royal Hotel to get my pre-game sleep. Butterflies, going nuts. Tonight was going to be my very first NHL play-by-play.

And then I got a phone call—it was Frank Selke Jr., the vice president of the Canadian Sports Network, the company that produced *Hockey Night in Canada* for the CBC, calling from Toronto.

"Bob, how are you doing?" he said. "What is your understanding about tonight's game?"

"What do you mean, my understanding?"

"What's your role?"

"I'm doing the play-by-play tonight. My first one."

"Bob," he said, "we're having some issues. I don't want to cause a problem for you, but apparently Mr. McDevitt has become upset with this."

In those days, the Montreal Canadiens—in the form of Sam Pollock, their general manager—had the last say in whoever the broadcasters might be.

"Bob has gone to see Sam Pollock and kicked up a bit of a ruckus because he doesn't want to do colour. He figures he's the voice of the Montreal Canadiens on the radio, so he has to do play-by-play of this game."

I told Frank that I didn't want to get caught up in this crap in the middle of the playoffs. I didn't want to cause problems and I didn't want to interfere.

"Do you mind?" Frank said.

"Don't worry. I don't want to interfere."

"Thank you very much, Bob, for your understanding. We'll be talking more."

I didn't say another word.

And so that was that. Over and done with. I wasn't going to go begging or anything. I backed off when I had to and minded my own business. But the truth is, when Frank Selke phoned me, it broke my heart.

I did the colour that night. McDevitt did the play-by-play. The Habs won game five. We'd be heading to the Boston Garden for game six.

After the game, Allan Gilroy called me in my hotel room and told me that he was going to have a meeting with Sam Pollock and get all of this resolved.

"You'll do play-by-play for the next game," he said.

The next day we flew to Boston and again they had the television meeting. After they were done, Ralph Mellanby came over to the three radio people and said, "Okay, we're not going to discuss this further. Cole, you're going to do the play-by-play tonight, and McDevitt, you're going to do the colour."

Needless to say, it was a tense meeting. McDevitt threw his arms up but Ralph shut him down.

"How many times have I told you we're not going to discuss it? That's it. Case closed."

AND SO I DID THE GAME—April 24, 1969, an afternoon game at the Boston Garden, my first NHL play-by-play. What a game to start with. It went to double overtime before Jean Béliveau scored the winner—the only overtime goal he scored in his career. It was history, and I was part of it. The Habs won the series, and they went on to sweep the St. Louis Blues in the finals and win the Stanley Cup.

Right after the game, we flew back to Montreal with the Canadiens on their charter. When I got back to the Mount Royal Hotel, there was a message waiting for me, telling me to call Allan Gilroy. He was delighted—and so was I.

"You can't believe the calls we got on the Toronto switchboard after the game, all positive," he told me. "You'll never work another game doing colour. You're on play-by-play from now on."

And that's how it was. I never did do colour on another game. Thank God.

Later, I was told that the Montreal Expos had been playing at Jarry Park that same afternoon as game six. The players kept stepping out of the batter's box and the pitchers were walking off the mound because they were distracted by the noise coming from the crowd that seemed to have nothing to do with the baseball game.

It turned out that it was the overtime, and people in the crowd were listening to my call of the Habs and Bruins on transistor radios and cheering when something happened. They wrote a story about it in the *Montreal Star*.

So the whole thing was working out pretty well for me. I was in. No turning back.

9

OH, BABY

The summer after doing my first NHL game, I was given a great assignment. CBC Radio was broadcasting the 1969 Canadian Open from Pinegrove, just outside Montreal, and I was one of the commentators. I love golf and have played for years. So that was terrific.

The CBC did sports on the radio only on weekends, and that year the tournament finished in a tie between Tommy Aaron and Sam Snead. They were going to play a full round on the Monday, but we weren't covering it. I wasn't doing the playoff. But I decided to stay and watch it. I went out early in the morning and watched Tommy Aaron hit golf balls on the range. There was nobody around. He was hitting and his caddy was out catching the ball on one hop with a baseball glove. He'd take another club and move back ten to fifteen yards and the caddy would catch it on one hop. Amazing. I was going out of my mind watching how accurate these guys were, sitting there all by myself on this little bank, when Tommy Aaron turned around and said, "How are you doing?" I said, "I'm doing marvellous. I'm amazed at your ball striking. Forgive me, but I've never been this close to a pro golfer. I'm doing the radio broadcast here." "I'm just loosening up," Tommy said. And then we got talking. He pulled out the three wood and the caddy backed up a bit. He was going on like that and the next thing I knew, who was warming up right over there but the great Sam Snead. What have I got going on here? So Tommy Aaron said to me, "Have you got an armband you use for radio?" (That was what they gave reporters as a pass so they could get inside the ropes on the golf course. I had one of those.) "Why don't you come and walk with us? You can walk with my caddy." So that's what I did. I walked the whole round and he won it on the eighteenth green with a decent putt and beat Sam Snead. And because Tommy Aaron was so kind to me, I paid no attention to Sam Snead for the whole three hours. Here was the swing of all swings in golf that I could have been studying, and I was hanging out with my new friend Tommy Aaron and enjoying every minute of it.

That turned out to be a pretty famous tournament in this country. The highlights were running on television one time, and I stopped to watch. There was Tommy Aaron sinking his putt on the eighteenth green. And who was walking around to shake his hand? Me. I didn't remember that until I saw it.

SO HOW DO YOU CALL a hockey game? That's a good question. I can only tell you how I do it.

It's not an easy job. An awful lot of work goes into listening to yourself, trying to get better. Even back when I was doing senior league games in St. John's, every Saturday night I would have my game taped. Then on Sunday, when I didn't work at the radio station, I'd go in and sit down and listen to the game from start to finish and make mental notes—did I do this or did I do that? And I kept searching for that flow, searching for that feel. Have I got it? If I haven't got it, why not? After a while it started to get better. It's coming, I thought. But I've never stopped trying to improve, even now, after all these years.

I can be an emotional person, so I don't find it very difficult to get involved in a game. I'm not sure if I could teach that. When I'm getting ready to do a game, I have butterflies. I've been doing it for many years but I still feel like that every time. There's nothing blasé about it. It must be like somebody going on stage. I can't speak for them. But I'm sure all performers have it. I don't like to call it nervous, but I'm pumped, waiting to get it going. And of course, you don't know what's about to happen. The game flows and I flow. How's it going to be tonight? I don't know. Don't ever tell me before the game that it should be a good one tonight. They don't go near me with that stuff. Oh, it's going to be a good one, is it? How do you know? Stop that. Let's hear the anthem and let's go. There it is.

I remember when I was calling the Western Conference final a few years back—Chicago and Los Angeles. A fabulous series. Went seven games. Darren Pang and I were having a meal before the game down in the press room, and he sat down with me and said, "Bob, I've got to ask you a question. Do you still get up before a game?" I told him, "I've got butterflies right now." He shook his head and said, "You know what? That's why it sounds like you're in it." And he's right. It's the same as when I used to walk in on the catwalk to the press box at the old Forum in Montreal. Even before I saw the ice, there was that burst of excitement that something was going on down below.

It doesn't really matter what the game is. It's all the same to me. It's still a hockey game. Now, to be honest, some games are tough to do because they're boring. The checking is close and there are no hits. Things are awful. But I've got to make it better, at least for the viewer.

WHEN I HAD my first chat with Foster Hewitt years ago, he told me some things to think about when you're calling a game. One of them is identifying players with teams. It's okay to say it's Sittler—everyone knows it's Sittler or Gretzky or Esposito. But little things like saying, "Doug Mohns of Chicago is coming out of his own zone. . . ." You need to keep everybody attuned because not everyone knows all the players—Foster was right about that. You're covering all your bases.

Between games, I try to watch as much hockey as possible, and that means I'm up late. There's a four-and-a-half-hour time difference between Vancouver or Los Angeles and St. John's. If I'm doing a game with a team I haven't seen before that season, I'll pick them up twice during the week. It's easier to get the games on television than it used to be. But it's not that easy keeping up with all the players. There are thirty teams out there.

A lot of people are pretty good at being critical, and I understand—it's the fan's right to be critical watching TV. But if you think about it, if you're doing a game with two teams that you haven't seen in quite some time—that's not an excuse, it's just reality—and then you have to be instantaneous with every move, it's tough. There's no two-second wait. You have to keep going. Flow with the game and help create the excitement for the fan watching.

If you've been in broadcasting as long as I have, you're bound to wind up making a little bit of history. And I guess that's what we did one night in the Boston Garden, when Harry Neale and I called the first network hockey game, ever, from another city from a monitor. They do it all the time in sports now. Sometimes, when it's the Olympics, the play-by-play guys are thousands of miles away in another country. But I think we were the first, though that certainly wasn't the plan.

It was an afternoon game in Boston. Jim Wilkes was in charge of our mobile units on the road, and he came to me while we were eating our pre-game meal and said he had to talk to me about something.

"I've been asked to come and see you," he said. "You don't have to do this, but think about it. If you're uncomfortable we'll find somebody in New York. After this game we're going to telecast tonight's game from Madison Square Garden, Washington against the Rangers. But because it was a last-minute decision to add the game, we don't have a crew there, so we want to set you up in the seats here with a monitor after the fans have left the building. You and Harry can watch the game on the monitor and call it as though you were there."

I said, "Don't get anybody in New York. I'll do it. It's a great challenge and I'm going to take this on. Here's what I'm going to need. I'm going to need somebody in the penalty box area of Madison Square Garden so that they can give me the time every two minutes—I won't have access to a clock. If anything unusual happens during the game, I have to get some information in my headset so I can pretend I'm there."

Finally it was all set up. They got Kathy Broderick from our office to go down to Madison Square Garden and got her set her up in the penalty box area. Jimmy Wilkes said he would be set up to talk to her and then they would relay what she said from our truck to my headset.

Harry and I sat in the seats and they got this small TV and taped it onto a couple of seats in the old Boston Garden. I did the game right from the start and it was great. Mark Askin was producing that night, and after four or five minutes he said, "Coley, it sounds like you're there." We really got flowing. Kathy was doing a great job and as much as I could I was making it sound like I was in New York.

Except for one thing. It was a one-goal game. Washington was leading New York and it was late in the third. A guy who was good for the Capitals around that time was John Druce. He got hot for a stretch and it was like he had goals coming out his ears that season.

I'm doing this game off the little monitor and the Rangers took the goalie out for the extra attacker—except no one told me.

All I saw on the monitor was that John Druce was coming out of the Washington zone and it looked like he was on a breakaway.

So I turned it up like you would for a breakaway, my voice getting more excited.

"It's John Druce! He's in all alone! . . ."

He skated across the blue line. And then the camera showed the empty net.

Oh my God. This is a joke.

It was pretty embarrassing.

THE TRUTH IS, you can do too much research. Think about the viewers now, sitting back with a beer and watching the game. They're pretty involved in this thing. You're not going to drown them with facts and stories. Let them watch the game.

In the playoffs, it's a bit different because you're totally wrapped up in the whole event. Jeez, at the Nagano Olympics, Harry Neale and I did eighteen games. Different teams. No break. Game this afternoon and another one tonight. It was fun.

No matter what game it is, I always go in thinking about how I'd be into the game if I was at home with the TV on. You're the voice in the fan's head, and you're either going to annoy that fan or help him or her enjoy that game. Hockey is the most exciting game in sports. Listen, I went to baseball games live in Boston and dozed off in the third inning—and I played baseball. I love the game. But there's nothing like hockey. And you have to feel what the fan feels.

I think I'm lucky to be able to sense that. I think I'm darned lucky. I think the best broadcasters out there have that same feeling about the game. But it can get you in trouble sometimes.

In March 1987 I was in the studio at Maple Leaf Gardens for one of the most famous—or infamous—moments in *Hockey Night in Canada* history, Dave Hodge's pen flip. We had just called the Leafs–Calgary game, which ended early. When that happened,

CBC switched the viewers over to a Montreal–Philadelphia game, which was tied late in the third period. That game finished tied, and so it was going to overtime. But the network decided that instead of sticking with it, only the viewers in the Montreal region would get the hockey. The rest of the country switched over to the regularly scheduled programming.

Dave was the host of *Hockey Night* then, and he went on air at the end of the game not knowing what they were going to do. Then someone told him through his earpiece what was happening, and he didn't like it.

I was sitting in a little room off to one side, watching it play out on a television monitor that was showing the CBC broadcast.

"Now, Montreal and the Philadelphia Flyers are currently playing in overtime, and . . . we are not able to go there," Dave told the audience. "That's the way things go today in sports and this network. And the Flyers and the Canadiens have us in suspense, and we'll remain that way until we can find out somehow who won this game, or who's responsible for the way we do things here. Goodnight for *Hockey Night in Canada*."

Then Dave picked up a pen and flipped it in the air.

I guess it was an awful thing to do on national television. But that's Dave. He's a man of principle. You have to admire that.

He refused to apologize, and so the CBC fired him. That was his last night on *Hockey Night in Canada*.

He was a very professional broadcaster—still is. And he was totally straight down the line in the way he worked. He treated his job seriously, like all good broadcasters should.

They brought in a guy from the west to replace him who we

didn't know much about—somebody named Ron MacLean. But in the end, I think that worked out okay. He came from Calgary, but was from Red Deer originally and worked in television out there. Don Wallace I think was our executive producer at the time and brought Ron in for a period of time to see if he could handle it. He was fantastic, boy. He had been doing the weather in Red Deer and with my flying I had to study meteorology and had done the weather for CBC in my own city, St. John's, so we had something in common and we talked a lot. We got to know each other early on and I was always a fan of his. I'm still a fan of Ron's. He's a true professional all the way and I admired him from day one.

And he's a great personality—a lot of fun. He and I got to be a little closer than most of the other guys. On any trips to New York I made sure we went to a Broadway show together. He didn't really get ensconced into the Don Cherry thing until later on. Even before that we had a lot of fun together. I really enjoyed his company.

ON GAME DAY, my routine is pretty set. For a Saturday night game, I get into town Friday night, flying in from my home in St. John's. I go over to the rink on Saturday morning and I want to see the coach. If I've never met him, I'll ask the team public relations guy if I can see him for a minute. If he's got a meeting with the players I'll wait around. I meet him and we chat for a little bit. I say, "Would you mind giving me your defence pairings and your four lines? It's just for me. If you don't want to name the starting goalie that's fine, but I'd prefer that you did." And then when I've got that, I go back to my hotel room.

The next thing I do is put the two team lineups on my cards—that's where you write down the players' names, their numbers, their positions, and the line and defence combinations. I've got my own way of doing things. It works for me. It's something I developed when I was doing games in Newfoundland starting in 1957. I've always done it the same way. I start with the goalie, then put the defencemen in front of the goalie and the lines in front of the defencemen. I've got the four lines going this way—left-centre-right, left-centre-right, left-centre-right, left-centre-right. I go to the defencemen—the right defenceman on the right side of the goalie, the left on the left. Some people say I do it backwards—Max McNab is the only NHLer I ever saw do it my way and we used to talk about that. But now some of the coaches are starting to agree with me, because when I'm up in the booth and I'm looking down that's the way I see it.

One time, I was working a game between the Leafs and the St. Louis Blues at Maple Leaf Gardens and staying at the old Westbury Hotel around the block. I came in the back door of the Gardens off Wood Street, and there was Mike Keenan standing right there. He was coaching the Blues at the time. We always got along great.

"How are you doing, Mike?" I said. "While I've got you here, do you have your lines set for tonight?"

"Sure," he said. "Do you have a pen?" And he gave me the whole works.

The Leafs were in the middle of their morning skate, so I waited for them to finish and then went into the dressing room, where all the press were talking to the players. I was looking for the coach, Dan Maloney. I pulled Dan aside and we sat down so that he could give me his lineup.

It's funny, I loved sports even before I became a Canadian. When I was a kid, Newfoundland was still ruled by Great Britain. Soccer (that's me in the middle of the back row) and rowing (that's me on the stroke oar) were huge in St. John's when I was growing up. And if I hadn't injured my leg playing soccer (or football, as we called it), I may never have got my first bike—or become fascinated by listening to hockey play-by-play as I lay in bed recuperating for five months.

I love the game of hockey, and I guess that comes through in my voice. The top photo is me in the broadcast booth at St. John's Memorial Stadium in 1957, my first year in broadcasting. Even back then, my line of work brought me into contact with legends of the game—here I am with Red Wings legends Alex Delvecchio and Gordie Howe. And I still love it. Here I am calling a game at the Air Canada Centre.

There may be nothing quite as exciting as calling a hockey game, but there are other things I love to do. I have always had the flying bug. Here I am in a Piper Cub in 1952. And years later, I was lucky enough to fly with the Snowbirds—and take control of the stick to perform a few maneuvers. I have also loved fly-fishing for many years.

Not all the professionals are on the ice. Over the years, I have been lucky enough to work with some truly great people. Here I am with Ron MacLean at my son Robert's graduation from Ridley College. Below that I am with the legendary Danny Gallivan, who helped me a lot when I was starting out. And here I am sharing a laugh with Don Cherry.

When you live and breathe the game for as long as I have, your professional life and your friendships really overlap. I am proud to call Glen Sather a friend, and it's safe to say that my career wouldn't have been the same without Harry Neale. One of my most memorable conversations with the great Toe Blake was about curling. He was just getting into the sport, and didn't know that I had skipped for Newfoundland at the Briar. I never won it, but Jack McDuff did, and he brought it over to my house. That's my dog Byng taking a drink from the tankard.

The players I've met over the years have been great guys. I can't say enough about Wayne Gretzky, who has always been generous and warm. That's him with my son, Robbie, on his twelfth birthday. Jean Beliveau was also always a true gentleman. His only overtime goal came in the first game I called. And below, here I am with true legends, Borje Salming and Al Arbour at our Hall of Fame induction. You can see the smile on my face a mile away.

No account of my career would be close to complete without acknowledging my children. Here I am on a trip with them to New York; I am pointing to the pier where my ship stopped on my first trip outside of Newfoundland. Below, there they are as young children: Hilary, Christian, Robbie and Megan. And here I am with my grandchildren, Gabrielle and Sam. I have been truly lucky.

In a sense, my career began when I first started listening to Foster Hewitt on the radio. And in another sense, it really began when I knocked on his door in Toronto years later, and he took the time to give a young stranger some advice. Here I am at his 80th birthday party—I was honoured just to be there. And here I am broadcasting from the booth named after him. I am honoured to be there as well.

Then Dan asked me who St. Louis was going to have playing on the first line that night.

"Dan, I can't tell you that."

"What are you talking about, Bob? I saw you over there talking to Mike."

"I'm sorry, but I can't. I'm sorry."

Dan was visibly upset. He wasn't very happy with me. So I apologized again and I left.

After the game I went down to our studio, which was right across the hall from the Leafs dressing room. And somebody came up to me and said Dan Maloney wants to see me if I had a minute. Holy cow. I wondered what was coming.

I went in to see Dan and he said, "Bob, I want to apologize to you. When I asked you about who Mike was playing, you didn't tell me, and that was the right thing to do. Now I know where you're coming from."

I thought that was fabulous. It made me feel like a million bucks.

Anyway, after I get the team cards done, I take a nap for a couple of hours. I've been doing it so long, they know my routine at the hotels where I stay. (It used to be the Westbury in Toronto right around the corner from Maple Leaf Gardens, before we moved to the Intercontinental near the Air Canada Centre. In Montreal, it's the Sheraton just up the block from the Bell Centre.) Nobody bothers me until four o'clock. The switchboard knows that. I tell them, don't forget now: no phone calls.

A few years back, they were having trouble putting the show together in the afternoon. They wanted to know something about the Leafs lineup. Somebody must have said, "Coley was here talking to the coach, so he'll know. Give him a call over at the Westbury." They had one of the assistants put in a call.

"Can I speak to Bob Cole, please?"

"I can't put your call through. Can you leave a message?"

"No, I've got to speak to him personally."

"Sorry, I can't put your call through."

Now, Ronnie Harrison was our producer then, and he was an excitable guy. The assistant told Ronnie that she couldn't get through to my room.

"Give me the phone," he said. "We've got to have him."

So he got on the phone to the hotel.

"Look, I'm the producer of *Hockey Night in Canada* with Bob Cole. Can you put me through? I've got to talk to him."

"No, sir, I can't put you through to talk to him."

"Excuse me? I'm Ron Harrison, the producer of *Hockey Night in Canada*. I NEED to talk to Bob Cole, our play-by-play man, right now."

"I'm sorry sir, I can't."

They wouldn't put him through no matter what he said. When I came over to the rink, they were laughing about it by then, but you could tell they were pissed off.

I've got my routine and I can't have it broken. Even my kids won't phone me between two and four. I'm out. And it works for me. I don't know what it does, but that's the way I have to do it.

Sorry, Ronnie.

The truth is, everybody has their habits. I remember when the great Dick Irvin somehow got us tickets to see Frank Sinatra when we were doing a game in Pittsburgh. Minnesota was in town, and they had turned over the Minnesota dressing room to Frank. When we got there early before the show, we were allowed to come in the room and look around at Frank's stuff. Jeez. Dick and I are big Sinatra fans. This is crazy.

I started asking one of Sinatra's people questions. He had Pond's tissues laid out. And he had Campbell's soup—it had to be Campbell's. The guy said that if he screwed up any of that stuff, he'd be gone, no ifs, ands, or buts. He wouldn't be working for him anymore. And when Sinatra comes in, everything stops, and you'd better be ready. At rehearsal, he'd walk up to the mike with his hat on and say, "Are you ready? Then give it to me." You'd better be ready.

So it's the same for me. That's the habit you're in. I wouldn't dare change it. What would I do that for?

After my nap I get up at about four, shower, get ready, and go over to the rink around five. I like to be in the booth an hour before the game. Get everything spread out. Maybe get a monitor moved or a microphone. Then I grab a meal in the press room—a little something, not much.

I'm fussy about the booth. This chair is too high, or not high enough. It's always a little different depending on the city. I arrange it so that I'm comfortable.

I like to hear the sound of the arena in my headset. I'm a bit fussy with whoever is doing audio on the game—and they know that. But they're great guys. They don't mind my coming into the truck and saying, now listen, can I get a little more? I'll tell them during the first period, can I get a bit more noise? Okay, Bob, we'll change it. And the directors are pretty good. They know I don't like to be busted up with stuff coming through my headset, so they ask me, do you want me to tell you when there's a commercial coming around? And I say no. Just tell me there's a commercial cue coming when I'm ready to go. I don't want to know thirty seconds before while I'm calling the action. Whatever you do, don't break my flow.

It's not just me. I remember a game in 1982 when Don Cherry was just starting out on television, and they had him doing colour. This was before they came up with Coach's Corner. They sent us out to Los Angeles to do a playoff game—the Kings versus the Edmonton Oilers, with Gretzky and everybody else, at the old Forum. The game wasn't even on our TV schedule. It was added last minute. Dan and I were hustled off to L.A. It turned out to be something special, one of the greatest comebacks ever. The Kings came back from 5–0 down to beat the Oilers 6–5. It was the third game of a best-of-five series, and Los Angeles wound up beating the Oilers in five. Kings fans remember that game as the Miracle on Manchester. Dr. Jerry Buss was the owner of the Kings in those days, and he gave up and went home before the comeback started.

But I think what I remember best was Don trying to do colour, and then stopping right in the middle of it.

With the mike open, right on air, he said, "Well, I'll be okay if this guy stops yelling in my headset while I'm trying to explain this thing." He was ticked right off.

As you can see, Don hasn't changed much.

I'VE WORKED WITH a lot of colour guys over the years, almost all of them ex-players or ex-coaches, and by and large they've been pretty good. Of course, I worked more games with Harry Neale than anyone else, and I think we had a pretty good chemistry in the booth. Everybody remembers us working together, but I'll bet there aren't many people who remember that I did games beside both Bobby Hull and Bobby Orr.

I remember doing a Montreal–Quebec playoff series one year with Bobby Hull as my colour guy. Boy, he knew how to play to the crowd. He was so popular. Everywhere he went he gave them that great smile, that great personality. He was flamboyant. And he liked doing the colour. He enjoyed the performing part of it.

Bobby Orr was the opposite. He was never comfortable in that role. Ralph Mellanby hired him for *Hockey Night in Canada* around the time Bobby was going from Boston to Chicago, and was injured so he couldn't play. We got along great, but he just never enjoyed the on-air work. Bobby didn't jump in that much, but he was terrific when he did get in. "Hey, this is Bobby Orr." I'd shut up and listen to Bobby Orr. Are you kidding? It doesn't get better than that.

We had a lot of fun together outside the booth. I remember one night we did a game in Edmonton. The next day he was flying to Chicago in the morning and I was going to Florida through Chicago, so we were going to be on the same early flight.

We were up in his room and having a few drinks, talking about hockey. It was terrific just passing time and having a talk with the great Bobby Orr. Here I am having a drink and here's Bobby Orr sitting in his shorts having a drink. And we're talking about hockey, passing the night away until we got on the plane in the morning. We never went to bed. Nothing to it but it was one of the greatest moments I can remember. He started telling me about his knee giving out, how he hoped it would get better but he'd played too long. I remember we tried to get ahold of Brad Park on the phone from the hotel room because Brad's knee wasn't good either and he also thought he'd have to quit soon.

Bobby told me all kinds of things. He told me about a time when he was playing in Boston, and he and Gerry Cheevers worked out a play that freed him up to take the puck up the ice. "I used to say to Cheesy, 'tell you what we'll do,'" Bobby said. "'I'll take the puck and go around the net and then I'll throw it back to you in the goal crease area.' I'd take off around the net to the right side. Cheesy would hang on to it a bit and then throw it up the boards on the right side to me going full speed. Nobody caught on to it, and I was gone." We used to laugh about it. Here was Bobby flying around the net. Nobody near him and no puck. Cheesy had the puck and then fed it to him with nobody near him on that side. Gone.

We talked about stuff like that, and here I am thrilled to death listening to Bobby Orr talking about how he played the game. But he never ever felt comfortable doing that on television because he didn't like to criticize other players even though nobody was as good as he was. He'd talk to me back at the hotel after, but he would never do it on the air. He had such great respect for everybody. He was so nice about it.

I'm probably hard to work with. But I don't think I'm a prima donna or anything. I just want to have it like this, and everybody in the right place. The colour guy has to be on this side of me. I can't be on this side of you.

There are a couple of things I'm very particular about. They're my quirks, I guess. One is that I don't like anyone to touch me when I'm working. The people around me know that, and they keep their distance. Don't ever come up and tap me on the shoulder during a game. The times that's happened—wow, it just throws me wild. I'm zeroed in, and when someone touches me, it's like I've been shot.

Wayne Gretzky did it to me once in Anaheim the year the Ducks won the Cup. Wanted to come up to the booth just to say hello. Harry Neale and I were doing the game. And somebody grabbed me by the shoulders and I just lost it. I looked around and there was Wayne. Hold it, that's okay.

THE OTHER THING that I do sometimes is hold my hand up to the colour guy. There are times when I want to play the crowd. Don't say anything now. Let the crowd go. I will tell the audio guy, if something happens like this and I'm saying this crowd is going crazy, give it to me and we won't say anything. Nothing we can say will improve on this. Let it go.

I think the main thing to recognize is that each of us has a tough job. We're going through a pretty gruelling situation here. We're live for two hours with no second chances. No re-recording. So we've got to help each other. The show is more important than us. The players are the stars. And we've got to make them sound like the stars. That's our job. I want the people watching us tonight to say, "Jeez, they're good. . . . That Jonathan Toews. I love the way he handles the puck." I don't want them talking about us.

Among the people I've worked with, there's no best guy, and they're all different. I'm sure they'd say the same about me—I'm different from so-and-so. It's hard to get totally comfortable with the guy you're working with.

But there's no question that Harry Neale was special. We had lots of terrific games together. He had a good feel for a game. He knew when to turn it up and when not to. You check out that gold-medal game at the Salt Lake City Olympics. I remember I met Ken Hitchcock, who was one of the coaches. Sometime after the next season started, he said to me, "Coley, did you ever sit down and listen to the gold-medal game?" I hadn't. "Well, you've got to get it. Get a tape of it. When I'm having a bad day I get that out and I stick it on and it makes me feel better."

So I sent off and got it. And I sat down one day and poured a drink and threw it on and listened to it. Jeez, I'm getting caught up in this game. It's a year ago and I'm getting all excited again. I said, holy cow, this is pretty good. I remember one goal—I guess it was Sakic's winning goal—I've heard that call many times. It was close until the last four minutes of the third period. We didn't know who was going to win this game. They got the goal and I said, "Surely that's got to be it. . . ." And Harry comes in right away with, "That's more than enough." He felt it all. You can't script that. Harry's voice was right there—"That's more than enough." It was just great.

Harry sees the game the way I do, and he lets it go. End-to-end stuff. Goalies are great. Shots are going off the elbow and stuff like that. He's not saying a word. He's just letting the thing happen. He doesn't jump in in the middle. Because when you do that you break the flow of the thing. You've got to grab the feel of the game and run with it. Hockey is exciting. Don't get in the way of it.

PEOPLE ARE ALWAYS asking me about "Oh baby!"—how I started saying that. The truth is, it just happened.

Years ago, when my daughter Megan was going to Ryerson University in Toronto, John Shannon, who was the producer then (and he was great at that job and continues now to work front and centre on hockey for Rogers), gave her a job working at *Hockey Night in Canada* during the playoffs. They were all asking her about the "Oh baby" thing, and she said, "What are you talking about? He's been saying that around the house as long as I can remember. He might say, 'Oh baby, what a great looking steak.'"

But the first time I remember it happening during a game was when Mario Lemieux did that wicked piece of stickhandling against Minnesota in the playoffs. I said something like, "Look at Lemieux, oh my, what a move." And then he pumped and scored and it was perfect timing, and "Oh baby" came out. It was a fluke.

Now, I say it if something on the ice makes me say it. You might hear an "Oh baby" or you might not. I don't really do it very much. I don't know when it's going to come out. No idea. But it happens. I remember a Tampa game with Vinny Lecavalier. He made a crazy bunch of stickhandling moves and scored and it happened. There's a little pause and then "Oh baby!" I don't plan it. It's spontaneous. I don't script the thing. It's ad libbed—and that's what broadcasting is all about.

The bottom line is you can't be boring. I don't want to blind everyone with stats and stories during the play. Lots of people like stories and that's great. But wait a minute—this is a hockey game. And there's stuff on the line here. Is this first place or third? It's got to be exciting. It's all about the voice. You've got to make your voice sound exciting in the right spots. Otherwise, what are you doing this for?

IT'S EXHAUSTING calling a game. When we're off-air during the intermission, I'll just sit back and catch my breath. We might shoot the breeze a bit in the booth. What did you think about that call? Stuff like that. I get the official stats that come up with about five minutes left before the next period starts. Shots on goal. Ice times for guys. It's there if I want to refer to it. Sometimes I eat it up and put it on the air. With a guy like Duncan Keith, for instance, you can't help but say, hey, he's going to hit thirty minutes tonight and he looks great now. As the game goes on you can't help saying things like that. It's part of the feel. But you don't want to overdo the numbers.

Then the period starts, and you're back at it. Stand by. Ten seconds. Bang. You're ready to go.

After the game, I'm drained. When we were still at Maple Leaf Gardens years ago, the producer of *Hockey Night in Canada* then, Ralph Mellanby, always had everybody get together for a drink after the game at the Hot Stove Lounge, just to wind down. But these days I usually go back to the hotel room, pour myself a drink, and try to unwind by myself. I can't get to sleep anyway. I've never been able to get to sleep right away. I just watch TV or read the paper and eventually go to bed.

There was a time when I used to stew over the broadcast. Jeez, why didn't I say that? I used to hurt myself. But you'll kill yourself if you keep that up. You have to walk away. It took me a while to learn that. No point in dwelling on it. It's done, gone. You can think you might have done better, but you can't dwell on it. It's live television and you have to understand that.

Then come Sunday morning, I'm on a plane back to St. John's.

10

1972

When I'm on the road, whenever I get the chance, I love to take in a show—especially if I'm in New York. I remember one time we were doing a series with the Rangers and I said to Ron MacLean, we're going out tonight. He said no, he wasn't interested—the boys were going out for Italian food and he was going with them.

"I've got two tickets for a Broadway show and you're coming with me," I said.

"I've never been to a Broadway show," he said.

"Well then, you're coming for sure."

So he reluctantly agreed to go with me. I had two tickets to Cole Porter's *Anything Goes*. We got there and we had great seats and we were talking to people as the orchestra was warming up. And the curtain rises and Ron looks at me, rolling his eyes, and I'm thinking, this isn't good. Then the orchestra comes in and he brightens up and in the end he loved it. He told me that he'd had the best night in New York that he could remember. We walked back to the Hilton, where we were staying, and all the guys were there and Ron was singing all these songs from *Anything Goes*. We had a marvellous time.

I ALWAYS CHECKED the papers in whatever town I was in just in case something good was going on.

On another trip to New York, there was this place right across from the hotel called The Blarney Stone—an Irish pub, and of course there are a million of those in Manhattan. Right next door to it there was a nightclub, and I found out that Sarah Vaughan was playing there.

Good God, I've got to see her. So I went in early and gave the guy at the door a couple of extra dollars and told him I wanted a good seat up front. Now I'm alone, and sat right up front—there was only a little dance floor between me and the stage. I was an hour early—one of the first people there. I'm sitting there all by myself. And the drummer of the band stood up and got into a heavy argument with somebody all the way across the room at the front door. The language was terrible. He was giving it to this guy and the guy was trying to explain something back to him but he wasn't listening. I learned later that this was the famous drummer Buddy Rich. Apparently, he had a reputation for that sort of thing.

Now that's over and the room has filled up and the show is going to start. The warm-up act for Sarah Vaughan is a comedian—Flip Wilson. This was before he had his own show on television and became pretty famous. So Flip comes out and he's got everybody going but I'm not really into it. I'm patiently waiting for Sarah Vaughan to come out and sing. I've got a great seat. It's perfect.

Flip was going on and on. And when he was finished he said, "I'm going to introduce you soon to the lady of the evening, Sarah Vaughan, but before I leave, I'm going to get this guy here laughing."

He comes down off the stage and he points right at me.

"I'm going to make you laugh."

It was a bit of fun. I guess I wasn't laughing. And I never did laugh.

Bring on Sarah Vaughan, or get me out of here.

ANYWAY, WHEN YOU'RE on the road all the time, year after year, you're going to cross paths with some interesting people. The strangest encounter of all left a lasting impression. A permanent one, actually.

We were doing the Boston Bruins–New York Rangers Stanley Cup final on radio in 1972. On the off-day between games in Boston, a group of us went out to dinner at a restaurant that's still around, called Pier Seven. Francois Carignan, our producer, was there, and so were Gilles Tremblay, René Lecavalier, and Lionel Duval, who were doing the French broadcast.

René and Lionel were staying at a different hotel, so on the way back they dropped us off at our place. We were standing outside the front doors and I went over to say goodbye to René and Lionel. As I was doing that, a scuffle broke out behind me.

I looked around and saw Francois involved in some kind of tussle with a guy who'd been standing outside the hotel having a cigarette. Holy cow! I ran back. Francois wasn't doing very well— the guy had him in a chokehold—so I jumped in and got Francois out of the way and then grabbed the other fellow and tried to restrain him. He was a decent-sized guy—over six feet tall and pretty strong. But I could always take care of myself. We were both tangled with each other and we stumbled around, and then the two of us crashed right through the glass door of the hotel and into the lobby. Bang. Glass flew everywhere.

Now we were on the floor and still holding on to each other. All of a sudden the hotel manager and other people were around us, and the police were there, too—it was as if they just came out of nowhere. They got us apart and everything was straightened away. My back was cut, and somebody decided that I'd better get to the hospital. The police had a paddy wagon outside, and I got in. Meanwhile, somehow the guy that I was fighting with had disappeared. Francois decided he was coming with me because I had helped him out. We went to Massachusetts General Hospital and I got thirty-some stitches in my back. It was a wicked night.

We came back to the hotel and everything had calmed down. Gilles was waiting for us in his room. He said the cops were around but he paid two hundred bucks for the glass that was broken and everything had quieted down, everything was resolved. It all seemed very strange, but that was the end of it.

We left for New York for the next game. I was sitting in my room when Gilles called me. "Have you seen the news?" he asked.

About three weeks before, a mobster named Crazy Joe Gallo had been murdered in New York. The gunmen opened fire while he was having dinner on his birthday at Umberto's Clam House. It was a famous crime—Bob Dylan even wrote a song about it. All kinds of shots were fired and Gallo wound up dying outside on the sidewalk. You'd think there would have been a whole bunch of witnesses, but somehow no one was ever arrested for the murder.

So Gilles had been watching the local news in New York and he said the story was something about a birthday and one of the underworld guys being knocked off. And the police were looking for somebody who they thought had gone to New England to hide out.

Gilles said, "The guy's picture was up on the TV screen, and I'm telling you, that was the guy who crashed through the window with you in Boston. I'm sure of it."

Now, I had my doubts about that. But after the game we left New York for Boston, and headed back to the same hotel. When I arrived it was drizzling. We pulled up to the hotel door. A guy came out with an umbrella and took my luggage and another guy came out with another umbrella and escorted me into the hotel. So this was different. When I got to the front desk there was no need to check in—they already had a room for me. I couldn't understand what was going on. It was like they knew me.

I went up to my room and it was a huge suite. A beautiful room. The best I'd ever seen in Boston. And then I got a call from my friend Gilles. "How's your room?" he asked. It turned out that they had done the same thing for him—walk-in closets, TVs all over the place. We were all set up in this hotel and we couldn't quite understand it. It was like they had been waiting for us to make sure we were looked after.

We started thinking about everything that had happened. Gilles was convinced that the guy on TV in New York was the guy who'd had Francois in the stranglehold. And why had the police turned up so quickly? It seemed like they were there in thirty seconds. How come everything quieted down so fast? I got back from the hospital and no one wanted any news about it at all. And then we got to the hotel the second time and it was as if they were waiting for us and making sure that we were looked after. It was a weird situation, and kind of scary.

Gilles and I talked about it for years. Francois must have said something or done something. And I was stupid enough to get involved—but in a situation like that, you do what you have to do.

And I've still got that scar on my back. My mafia scar. It's quite the souvenir.

I REMEMBER WHEN I first heard the news. The Leafs were playing the Bruins at the Boston Garden and I was doing the game for Sunday night radio on CBC when the word got out that Russia was going to play Canada in a series the following September. Harold Ballard was in the building that night, and we got him on the air and interviewed him between periods about it, talking about how the NHL was finally going to put a team together and beat the Soviets. They had won all those world championships and Olympic gold medals. Now Canada was going to send its best players against them. Pretty much everybody thought that the NHL players would win, and win easily.

So the buildup started. That summer—August 1972—I was asked to host the CPGA tournament in Ottawa on radio with Nick Weslock doing colour, working on the eighteenth green. Jeez, I'm into heavyweight stuff now. I had to bluff my way through it as if I knew what I was doing. I met Bob Panasik and he was great with me. In the end, he won the tournament. That Sunday afternoon, the last day of the golf tournament, we got word that CBC Radio had obtained the rights to cover the Summit Series (remember, CTV had the series on television). I was told by Allan Gilroy, who was the head of CBC Radio Network Sports, that I'd be doing the play-by-play and Fred Sgambati, who worked out of Toronto, would be doing the colour.

That 1972 series was the biggest thing that ever happened to me in broadcasting. At the time, it was the biggest thing ever—and for Canadians old enough to remember, it still is.

And why me? What did I do to get this? That's crazy. I remember when I got word that I'd be calling the series, I went back to my hotel room and looked at myself in the mirror and said, where are you going?

When I was eleven years old, I was in bed with a sore knee pretending I was Foster Hewitt, and now here I was going over to Russia.

Are you joking?

WE GOT CALLED DOWN to Toronto for all the briefings and to do the visa application stuff and get our clothing taken care of, around the time that Team Canada was holding its training camp at Maple Leaf Gardens. That's when Gilroy called me into his office over on Jarvis Street, where the CBC headquarters used to be. "Now, Bob, I've got to tell you I'm having some problems here in Toronto," he said. "You know that Freddie is the lead sportscaster here for CBC Radio. . . ." It turned out that Sgambati had come to talk to Allan and told him that he wanted to be the play-by-play guy for the Summit Series. He'd done some of the Sunday night NHL games for CBC Radio, the same as I had.

"I've got trouble here," Gilroy said. "Freddie wants to do the play-by-play. I had decided that you'd be the play-by-play guy and Freddie was going to be the colour. What do you say we split it—you do the play-by-play of the four games in Canada, and Freddie does the play-by-play of the four games in Moscow?"

I nearly ended my career right then and there.

I said, "You know what, Allan, that's not very professional. If we're going to split it, it must not be that important. And I think it's very important. So if you want Freddie to do it, go ahead. He can do the eight of them. I don't want to do that. I'll bow out."

He was so angry that he threw his pencil across the desk. But in the end he came over to my side. He said, "Bob, you're doing the play-by-play on the games here and in Russia. That's the end of that." I told him I was a little uncomfortable now. "Don't be," he said. "You're it, and that's it, okay?"

So that was it.

Now fast-forward to September. The series was starting in Montreal the next Saturday. I got cramming like I always do, trying to learn as much as I could about the Russians. I had to get ready for this baby. There were twenty-six names on the potential Soviet team. I had to get them—and I did somehow. All twenty-six names. But I still needed to find out how to pronounce them.

I learned that the Soviets were going to be landing on Wednesday in Montreal, three days before the first game at the Forum. So I phoned Gilroy in Toronto from my home in Newfoundland and said, "Allan, I'd like to get a head start." We were scheduled to travel to Montreal on Thursday or Friday to get ready for the Saturday opening. I wanted to go Wednesday. "Well, that's kind of early, Bob," he said. "It's expensive with the hotel and every-thing." I told him that if it came down to that, I didn't mind paying the difference myself, but I had to go down there and get accustomed to what I was going to have to do. "You know what?" he said. "You're thinking right. We'll make sure you get your room." They got me in the Château Champlain, just down the street from the Queen Elizabeth Hotel, where the Russians were going to be staying.

I found out what time their plane was arriving, and I got the name of the official Soviet interpreter, a fellow named Viktor. There was a Canadian translator—Aggie Kukulowicz, who worked in Winnipeg for Air Canada. But I wanted to get the Soviet guy. I wanted to get *their* guy.

I was waiting when the Russian team bus arrived in front of the Queen Elizabeth. I don't remember seeing any other reporters. The Russians all got off that bus and—I can remember it like it was yesterday—they all looked the same. Not a smile. Nothing. They all wore dark clothes. They all got off and walked straight ahead behind the leader guy. And he went in and they followed behind him and didn't speak to a soul. They walked by me and, my God, I was scared to death. You have to remember this was 1972.

Then I met Viktor, and I sat down with him and went over the names. It turned out that he was a great guy. I had a winner here. He had studied English at Oxford University.

We had breakfast together at the Queen Elizabeth and went through all the names. I would point to a name and he would pronounce it, and then I'd write it down phonetically. When we were done, he said, "Let's meet in two days and go over them again." I pinned up a piece of paper with the names and the pronunciations on it in my hotel room and studied them. I lived and ate the twenty-six names for two days. Eventually I had them all down to a science—every single one.

Two days after our first meeting, I sat down with Viktor at the Queen Elizabeth for breakfast. He said, "Okay, Bob, I'm ready. Let's see you go. . . ." I had the list in front of me. Bang, I started off. Lebedev, Tretiak—all of them right through the whole bunch. He didn't say a word. He let me go on. I kept looking at him for a sign. Then, when I got to the end, he hit his hand on the table. "Perfect! Every one!" he said.

I also got Viktor to introduce me to the Soviet coach, Vsevolod Bobrov. A lot of people have forgotten about him. They remember Anatoli Tarasov, who came before him, the guy they called the father of Soviet hockey, and Viktor Tikhonov, who came after. But the Soviets brought Bobrov in to coach their national team in the Summit Series. It turned out that Bobrov was a pretty interesting guy. He started out as one of the greatest soccer players in the history of the Soviet Union. It wasn't until he was on a tour of England with Moscow Dynamo just after the war in 1945 that he saw indoor ice hockey for the first time—the game he and the other Russians played on ice before that was bandy, which was always played on an outdoor rink. Bobrov went on to become one of the greatest Russian hockey players ever. He played on world championship and Olympic gold-medal teams, and back in the 1950s, Rocket Richard said that he was one of the best players in the world.

The big Russian sports broadcaster then was a guy named Nikolai Ozerov. He called all the hockey games from ice level. (I actually tried to get Ozerov to come up and use one of the spare booths in the Forum to call the first game in Montreal. You can't do it down there, I thought. Nope. He wouldn't hear of it. He wanted to do it down there just left of the bench with his nose up against the glass.) In Russia, Ozerov was held in high esteem, almost as if he were part of the team. When Viktor the translator introduced me to Bobrov, I think Bobrov decided that I must be Canada's answer to Ozerov, so immediately he treated me with great respect. Right from the start we got along pretty well.

Bobrov didn't speak any English, but we got into this thing where he'd say *nyet* or *dah* as I went through his lineup, asking him who he was going to use. It was beautiful. It felt like we were friends.

The Team Canada dressing room was open to anybody in the media. Reporters and broadcasters could just walk in. But nobody was allowed to go into the Soviet dressing room—except me. When we got to Moscow there were even Soviet soldiers guarding the door. But when Bobrov saw me standing outside, he would say, "Come," and the army guys would move aside and let me in.

I remember the first time I went in, all their equipment was piled up in the middle of the floor. The guys had come in off the ice straight-faced, all business. It was a frightening, frightening thing. I was scared to death. They were going to beat us. And they were so serious. They all picked up their gloves and their pads and went to their lockers.

My last memory of Bobrov came after a game most people don't remember. Following the four games against the Russians in Moscow, Team Canada flew to Prague to play an exhibition game against the Czechoslovakian national team before heading home. After that game we went back to our hotel, and we were sitting in the lounge at a big table—George Duffield, Fred Sgambati, me, and maybe one or two others. We were having a beer when someone said to me, "There's a guy over there standing up and waving at us." He was way over on the other side. It was Bobrov. He was standing up and looking for me and he had his glass up. I'll be goddamned. So I got my glass up and we toasted across that big room. Jeez, can you believe this guy?

It was a wonderful thing to see after all that, and after his team lost. I was his only connection with Canada, it seemed. And he was standing for so long with the toast. People were applauding. It was a nice moment.

Bobrov died a few years later in a car accident. I've never forgotten how good he was to me.

NOW BACK TO THE SERIES. It was Saturday night and we were at the Montreal Forum. I'd been saying those names in my sleep. George Duffield was our radio producer, and he and I were in the booth together. Prime Minister Trudeau was to drop the puck for the ceremonial faceoff and we were getting ready for the game. The warm-up was on. Team Canada and Team Russia. I was just watching them and started warming up off-air by calling what I was seeing: "Petrov takes the puck and flips it into the corner, and Tysgankov feeds the puck and gets it out. . . ." Then Fred Sgambati said, "Hold it, hold it. . . ."

"What?"

"What did you say for number seven?"

"I said Gennady Tsygankov" (I pronounced it the way Viktor had taught me—Se-*gone*-kov).

"No, no, no," Sgambati said. "That's *Sig*-in-kov."

I said, "Excuse me, Freddie. Believe me, I worked hard at this. It's Se-*gone*-kov."

"Well, I'm telling you it's *Sig*-in-kov. I had him as a junior in a tournament in Salt Lake City and it's *Sig*-in-kov. And that's what I'm using."

George Duffield overheard us arguing and asked what was the matter. Freddie said, "We've got a disagreement here. Bobby is calling this guy the wrong name, the wrong pronunciation, and we're not having that." George asked me what I was calling him and I told him, "Se-*gone*-kov," and Freddie said, "No, it's *Sig*-in-kov."

George told me to go along with Freddie because he had called games with the Russians before.

I said no.

"Bob, I'm telling you—"

"And I'm telling *you*, George, I'm here now and I'm doing this game and every time he has the puck it's going to be Se-gone-kov. And if you don't like that I'm going home tomorrow. Freddie can have it all. I'm finished. I can't go on the air and say something that I know not to be right."

Sgambati was delighted because there was an uproar going on. I could tell. But I said that's it. I'm finished. Gone. It took some nerve for me to do that, but it was the principle of the thing. I had worked so hard on those names. I just can't do this. So I'm going home. I'm going home after game one. That's it.

Claude Mouton was the famous public address announcer at the Montreal Forum. Now it was time for him to introduce the players. First, it would be Team Soviet Union. Mouton got to number seven—"Gennady Se-*gone*-kov."

I said, "Did everybody hear that?"

Freddie gave me the finger.

I thought, holy Christ, what a way to start this. But I said to myself, Robert, you're here, be sensible. You've got that little thing taken care of. From now on they're going to take your pronunciations. Pay attention. Calm down. Just do your work.

And that's what I did.

I've got to give Fred credit. When we did the exhibition game in Prague at the end of the series, we were walking across the parking lot outside the rink to our hotel. And Sgambati said, "Coley, I want you to stop a second. I want to shake your hand."

He was pretty nice with his compliments and it all ended great. But the truth is, I nearly went home before the series started.

OF COURSE, all of that was beside the point compared to what was happening on the ice. As I said, I was doing the radio play-by-play for CBC, with Sgambati doing the colour. The television broadcast was on CTV, with Foster Hewitt coming out of retirement to do the play-by-play and Brian Conacher as his colour man. Brian had played for the Maple Leafs, but he'd also played for Father Bauer's national team, so he had experience playing against the Russians.

Team Canada got a 2–0 lead quickly in that first game at the Forum, and then she just changed. The Soviets were obviously in better shape. Skating faster. Our guys were a step slower. I couldn't figure it out. Ken Dryden was the goalie and they were just beating him. It was unreal to see it unfold before my eyes. I was in tears at the hotel after. I had seven more games to do and had been living for this once they told me I was doing it. It was going to be a huge moment in my career. But now it looked like we were dead.

Two nights later, Canada won in Toronto, then on to Winnipeg, where they were leading, but the game ended up tied. Then we got to Vancouver and lost and the crowd was booing—and that's where Phil Esposito made his famous speech.

The next day we were leaving for Stockholm, Sweden, where Team Canada would play two exhibition games, and then another one in Helsinki, Finland.

Getting on that plane for Europe, everybody was in shock. Honestly, I don't know what we were thinking. This was going to be tough, going over and trying to beat those guys. It wasn't so desperate after the first game in Montreal because we won in Toronto and might have won in Winnipeg. But after Vancouver, the mood was bad.

On the way over, we stopped in Paris for half a day. Some of the guys wanted to go to downtown Paris and have a drink outdoors, but I wasn't into that. Then we flew on to Stockholm.

That's when I think the Canadian team finally got down to business. They might not have taken the Soviets that seriously to begin with, but now they knew how good they were.

But first they were going to be playing against the Swedes. We had heard a lot about their stick work. There's no fighting, but look out, they're terrible with their sticks. In that first game, one of the Swedish players got his stick right in Wayne Cashman's mouth and ripped his tongue open. He showed it to me after and it was cut right down the middle. It was an awful-looking thing. Cashman couldn't play in the second game in Stockholm because they couldn't stitch his tongue together, so I invited him to watch in the booth with me. That's when we bonded and became lifelong friends.

Then it was on to Helsinki, and finally Moscow, where they put us in the Intourist Hotel close to Red Square.

The first thing I did after we landed was head out to the Luzhniki Arena, where the games were going to be played. I always wanted to see the booth in the rink before I called the game because I wanted to be comfortable. I went into the booth and saw that Foster would be down to my left with Brian Conacher. You had to climb down into it a step or two, and jeez, it wasn't very big. But I could see the ice okay. Right in front of us was the roof of a big bandstand. They told us that was the area reserved for the hierarchy of the Soviet government. That's where they would be sitting, and that's why it was protected.

The radio booth had sections of glass all around it, and I realized I wasn't going to be able to hear very much of the sound from the arena. I couldn't have that. I had to get the glass out of there. So I got out of the booth and climbed down a few steps and out onto the roof above the area where the guys from the Kremlin were going to be. I looked up at the glass, and sure enough there were a couple of screws that I could take out. We had a Soviet lady who was responsible for us. Through the interpreter I asked her how I could get the glass taken out. "We can't, we can't," she said, which was no surprise. But I said I had to get it taken out. I told George Duffield, "I can't do a game like this in a closed-in booth. I've got to get the glass out." He said, "Take it easy. We'll take care of it." But the lady kept saying, "No, no, we have no workers available to take it out."

Back at the hotel, I told Dick Beddoes the story—he was there covering the series for the *Globe and Mail*. I told him I was going to take the glass out myself that night. I got a screwdriver from somewhere. That glass was coming out.

Beddoes said, "I'll help you."

So that night we went down to the stadium before the game. He climbed down on the roof and I went into the booth and we loosened all the screws without anyone noticing. Now it was just before the game. The warm-ups were over. I gave Beddoes the screwdriver and we finished taking out the screws. Then I pushed the glass out and he caught it.

Instantly about six army guys showed up and grabbed the glass and pushed him away. They put the glass back up. Screwed it back up and left me closed in. They couldn't find anyone that morning to take the glass out. Now, bang—they've got six guys to put it back in. That's the way it was over there.

I did the whole first game with that frigging glass sealing in the booth. It was awful. Then we had a meeting with this guy and another guy and the stadium manager—a big army woman. They finally agreed to take it out. So they took it out for the last three games.

I GOT TO KNOW some of the players over there really well because we were staying in the same hotel. Remember, I'd only been doing NHL games since 1969, so I was still pretty new to it. I remember running into Frank Mahovlich in Moscow. You've probably heard the stories about how he thought the Russians were spying on him and had bugged his room. I remember asking him, "How are you doing, Frank?" and he said, "I feel strange."

"Are you playing tonight?"

"I don't think so," he said. But I guess they talked him into it. You've got to remember, it was a frightening time.

Don Awrey, who played beside Bobby Orr on the Boston defence, had been benched after the first game in Montreal, when Valeri Kharlamov skated around him and scored a goal. Don didn't get back in the lineup. His wife didn't make the trip (my wife was there, but she was busy with a tourist group). So we ended up spending a lot of time together, walking around Red Square after practices, and we got to be friends. He was a great guy. I remember looking across the arena during one of the games and seeing the guys who weren't playing wearing their red team jackets—Awrey, Mickey Redmond, Vic Hadfield, the others who didn't walk out on the team and go home. I invited Don to come up and squeeze into the booth with me to watch the games.

Don was with me during the eighth game. Remember, it was 5–3 for the Soviets after two periods. During the intermission, Sgambati was doing interviews, so we climbed down from the booth for a smoke. We weren't alone. It seemed like all of the Soviets were smoking.

I remember saying to him, "This looks like curtains. I don't think they can come back from 5–3." I asked Don what he thought was going on down in the Team Canada dressing room. He said, "I'll tell you what's going on. They're all saying the same thing. We've got to go out and just give 'er as soon as they start the period, and then see what happens. This two-goal lead has got to go."

That's exactly what happened. A little over two minutes into the third period, Phil Esposito scored the goal to make it 5–4, Yvan Cournoyer tied it up ten minutes later, and the rest is history.

Paul Henderson scored, and I said whatever I was going to say. Hearing Foster's call—"Henderson has scored for Canada!"—it was wicked. I don't think my call was as good as Foster's, but I've heard it was okay. People liked it. I hope they did enjoy it.

This is how I called the last seconds of that game for CBC Radio:

Esposito upended as he tried to shoot it. Here's another shot. Henderson right in. He scores! Henderson! [the crowd roars] And Kenny Dryden. I've never seen a goaltender skate that far from one end of the rink to the other. And the team officials are over the boards. Henderson has got to be the hero of an entire nation now. Thirty-four seconds left. They've got a 6–5 lead. Can they hang on? It's almost unbelievable coming from behind against this really, really fine Soviet hockey team. It was 5–3 going into this period. Esposito scored at 2:27, Cournoyer at 12:56, and now Henderson, who was the hero of the seventh game, scoring with just thirty-four seconds left. Esposito will undoubtedly get an assist—he has been given an assist, I understand. He was in there fighting for it but Henderson was the man who knocked it in. They drop at centre ice now. Team Canada leading 6 to 5. It goes back to the Russian blue line. Kuzkin going back for it. Gives it to Gusev. Gusev a pass on the right side for Mikhailov. He shoots it in. Twenty seconds left. They're trying to clear it. Gets it through the middle down the ice. It's wide of the net and it's not called icing. Somebody could have played it. Twelve seconds left to go. Russia on the move. Here they come. Petrov coming out. And it's Gusev trying to get around. Off the boards. Dryden takes it. Three seconds left. THE SERIES IS OVER!

I was pretty excited myself. I was caught up in this baby, too. The final period of the final game and now the goal . . . I'm on top of the world.

When it was all over I stopped and I looked at Don and he was crying. Not saying a word. Tears running down his cheek. Boy, what a moment. And I'm all shaken up now. It was unreal.

There can never be another game like that. The Salt Lake City gold-medal game was terrific. First gold medal in fifty years. But with that Summit game there was so much tension for a month. Nobody can ever get that feeling again.

I HAVE TO TELL YOU a funny little story about what happened right after the last game in Moscow. Not a lot of people remember it now, but that actually wasn't the last game in the series. As I said before, Team Canada went from there to Prague, where they played an exhibition game against the Czechoslovakian national team before heading home.

In those days, when you visited one of the communist countries in the old Eastern bloc, there was an official exchange rate for the local currency—and then there was the unofficial rate you could get on the street through the black market. When we were there, the official rate was six korunas—the Czechoslovakian currency—to the dollar. But you could do a lot better than that if you went looking.

When we got to Prague, I asked a taxi driver about it. He said that he might be able to get me sixteen or seventeen to one. Another driver told me he could introduce me to a guy who could get me twenty-six or twenty-seven to one.

Well, I'm going to take this. How am I going to do it?

The guy said he'd make a phone call and arrange for his buddy to meet me. Now I've got a whole clandestine operation going on.

My friend Red Fisher, the great sportswriter from Montreal, was on the trip, and I told him about it and immediately he was scared to death. "I can't do this," he said. "I've got to come back here. I might not be allowed in the country."

"You leave it with me," I told him.

Everybody from Team Canada was going to this famous crystal store. I don't know anything about crystal, but apparently the Czechs are pretty good at handcrafted crystal. Glasses and vases and things.

But first I met the money guy. He turned up on the corner of a cobblestone street in the middle of Prague. It was very secretive. I got Fish to give me two hundred dollars—he was reluctant, but finally he gave it to me. I threw in another two hundred and we wound up with thousands of korunas. Fish was still really scared to death with this. What was I getting him into?

We went to the store and we had to go upstairs to this big showroom where all the magnificent crystal was. I remember Pete and Frank Mahovlich were buying this and buying that.

I was just walking around admiring the work and noticed this beautiful vase. It was red and gold and had silver beads and was all handcrafted. Beautiful. Harold Ballard came by and saw me looking at it and said, "Robert, are you buying that vase?" I didn't intend to buy the vase. I said, "What are you talking about, Harold? You going to buy that?"

I could see that he took a shine to it. I had no idea how much it cost and I didn't know a thing about crystal, but after Harold said that I decided to buy it. "Well, if you change your mind, I'm going to buy it," he said. I got it—I turned over a big pile of my black market korunas and had it packed.

I'm glad I did. I still have it at home. It's a great conversation piece. And it's a nice memory of the Summit Series, and of Harold, who was a good friend.

WE HAD SOME IDEA of what was going on back home in Canada while we were in Moscow. There were all the telegrams and wires posted on the wall of the Team Canada dressing room, and we were hearing stuff from our families. So we knew it was a pretty big deal. We were scheduled to fly out of Prague and then land in London to refuel. From there we'd fly on to Montreal, where Prime Minister Trudeau was going to welcome the team home, then on to Toronto, where there'd be a big parade downtown.

What a flight that was. What a party.

As we were crossing the Atlantic, I went up front to talk to the pilots. I was going through the flight plan and the rest of it. We were over Greenland and they told me that soon we'd be flying over St. John's. That was a checkpoint for the pilots after they crossed the ocean.

So I said, "You know what, I should send a message down from Team Canada. All of Canada is waiting for the airplane to come—they're coming home. How about turning on the PA to the cabin back there and I'll do something?"

I got on the PA system. "Okay, I want everybody to pay attention to what I'm saying here." Remember, there's a big party on that plane. "I've got news for all you guys back there. We're now over St. John's, Newfoundland, and so this is Canada!" I could hear everyone cheering.

We got hold of the tower in St. John's and the pilot told them he had Bob Cole in the cockpit. "Can we send a message to Canada from the flight letting people know that the team is getting close to Montreal?" CBC Radio patched it through. I'm not sure where it aired but it was big stuff—Team Canada coming home after a month like that.

I went back to my seat. Harold Ballard was sitting right in front of me. He always called me Robert and insisted that I call him Harold.

"I'm coming to Newfoundland if I have to and we're going to get you up to Toronto," he told me. "We're going to get rid of those Hewitts and you're going to be my guy."

Well, that was a little embarrassing.

A few minutes later, I was still talking to Harold, who was sitting next to his son Bill—who later became a well-known concert promoter. Alan Eagleson walked up the aisle and stopped by our seats. He was with Bobby Orr.

People forget that Orr was part of that team. He was coming off one of his many knee surgeries, but he had hoped to play. He skated with the team during their training camp in Toronto, and gave it another try before the games in Sweden. But he just couldn't do it. A lot of people think the series might not have been so close if he'd been able to play for Canada. And I always thought the world of Alan. He was great to me.

Eagleson and Orr stopped in front of me to talk to Harold. And that's when Bill Ballard piped up.

"You made us ashamed," he said to Eagleson. "You shamed Canada. You embarrassed us all."

He was talking about that moment in the series when Eagleson complained about the officiating and Soviet officials hauled him across the ice, and then he flipped a middle finger at the goal judge at the Soviets' end of the rink.

Orr wasn't having any of that. He got right in Bill Ballard's face, defending Eagleson.

"If your dad wasn't here," he said, "I'd punch you right in the nose."

That was the end of it. Eagleson and Orr moved along, and Harold turned to Billy and said, "You don't know when to keep your mouth shut, do you?"

Then Harold looked over to me and said, "How are you doing, Robert?"

It was all over quickly.

LET ME TELL YOU a little bit about Harold Ballard, because I had a different experience with him than a lot of people did. He had a terrible reputation with the media and the fans when he owned the Maple Leafs, and of course a lot of those teams were awful on the ice. But I got to know him pretty well.

I remember one time I was at the Gardens for a morning skate, and I heard him holler my name.

"Robert!"

There was Mr. Ballard, up at the top of the section where we were sitting.

"Come up." So I walked up the steps, and he asked me if I had a minute, and then led me down the hallway. He took out his keys and he opened this door—I didn't know there was a door there.

"C'mon in."

And now I was in his apartment. It was where he lived, right inside Maple Leaf Gardens. (I remember when I told Don Cherry this story, he couldn't believe it. "You were in his apartment? Nobody goes in his apartment.") We had a chat about things— hockey, broadcasting. He liked my work. It was great.

THERE WAS ALSO another side to him. When my son, Robbie, was about six years old, he had a medical problem and I happened to mention something about it to Harold. We were in St. Louis for a game and he'd asked me, "How is that little boy of yours?" I told him about the issue Robbie was dealing with.

I went into the press room for the pre-game meal, and Bob Stellick came up to me—he was the public relations man for the Leafs in those days. "Mr. Ballard wants to see you down by the Leafs dressing room," he said.

I got down to the dressing room and there was Harold with the team doctors.

"We're going to look into whatever it is with your little boy and get it straightened out," he said. When I tried to object he said, "Don't you talk to me. We're getting this going."

On Monday morning I got a call telling me that Harold had been in touch with one of the top specialists at the Hospital for Sick Children in Toronto and Robbie was to come up and see him. That's what we did. In the end, things turned out fine for Robbie.

That's what Harold did for my boy.

Any time I hear people talking about Harold in a derogatory sense, I feel like standing up and saying, hold it. You don't know everything about that man. I knew a side of Harold that a lot of people didn't.

Later on I took Robbie to Toronto with me, and took him down to the bunker to meet Harold in person. Harold called him in and sat him on his lap. There's a great picture of Robbie and Harold together.

I'd go to bat for Harold Ballard no matter what.

SO BACK TO THE FLIGHT. We landed in Montreal and everyone was pretty dishevelled at that point. It had been a long flight and they had played hockey the previous night in Prague and partied the night before that after the last game in Moscow. It was going to take everybody a little while to get presentable so they could meet the prime minister.

The airplane rolled up the tarmac at Dorval Airport, and a fire engine was waiting and so were the crowds. Thousands cheering like you wouldn't believe. It was quite a scene. I got off first with that red CBC Radio jacket on and this guy yelled at me, "Excuse me, excuse me. Can you come here for a moment?"

Now, Yvan Cournoyer, the two Mahovlichs, Red Fisher with the *Montreal Star*, and I were leaving the airplane there. The Montreal guys were going home and I'd be catching a flight to St. John's the next day. The rest were going on to Toronto, where there would be a parade to city hall. I'd been gone for a month. I wanted to get home. Then this guy called me over. His said his name was Victor Chapman. It turned out he was the prime minister's press secretary.

"Bob, you know all the players, right?"

Well jeez, I hope so.

"You've got to come with me," he said. "We need somebody to introduce the players to the prime minister."

What? Okay, I guess.

So I walked with him through the crowds and past the RCMP, and there was Pierre Elliott Trudeau. Victor introduced me to him.

"Welcome home. Nice to meet you," Mr. Trudeau said. "I've heard some of your work."

He was very polite and proper as we waited for the players to get off the plane. I remember saying to him, "You've got a great country here, sir." He said, "Yes, I know." It turned out that someone had cut Cashman's pants off, so they had to try to find him clothes. It was an awfully long wait. But I had a great time with the prime minister.

"You're from Newfoundland?"

"Yessir," I said. "I'm going home tomorrow. I'm staying here at a hotel tonight and then flying to St. John's in the morning."

"No, you're not," Mr. Trudeau said. "You're going home tonight." Excuse me?

They were in the middle of an election campaign, you see. And he had his own airplane, a Viscount. They were heading for Newfoundland that night.

"You're coming home with me," he said. "Victor, get Bob's bags and put them on our airplane and set him up with a meal and whatever he wants. He's coming home with us."

Finally, the players came down from the plane and I introduced them to the prime minister. Then I flew home with Mr. Trudeau on his plane. I was totally blown away by his gesture.

When we landed in St. John's all the Liberals in Newfoundland were at the airport to meet the prime minister—and I was the first one off the plane. I didn't know I'd be getting that kind of welcome.

11

BACK TO THE USSR

Two years after the first Summit Series, I was back in the Soviet Union, doing the CBC Radio play-by-play of the games between the Russians and a new Team Canada assembled from players in the World Hockey Association. That series has been kind of lost to history for some reason—maybe because it fell right between the '72 series and the first Canada Cup in 1976, maybe because the WHA was never regarded the same way as the NHL, or maybe because that time we lost—though the games were very close. The series was tied after the four games in Canada, and then the Russians didn't lose a game on home ice.

You couldn't do another one like '72, but it was a good attempt and it was a close series. And there was plenty worth remembering, starting with the fact that Gordie Howe was there and Bobby Hull was there. It was exciting from that point of view. There were some other good players as well, including Frank Mahovlich and the hero of '72, Paul Henderson, who were both playing for the Toronto Toros. Everybody got into it.

Hull had been barred from the '72 series because he left Chicago and signed with the Winnipeg Jets of the World Hockey Association. So this was his first chance to play against the Russians, and Bobby was in his prime. He was great with the fans. The bus had to wait all the time for Bobby to sign all of the autographs and get aboard. He was voted the most popular player on Team Canada by the Russians and won a trip to some famous resort on the Black Sea. Whether he ever took the trip, I don't know.

Gordie Howe was past his prime at age forty-six but could still deliver—he finished fourth in scoring in the series, ahead of the great Russian star Valeri Kharlamov, and played alongside his sons Mark and Marty. I remember out in Vancouver when we had the last game in Canada, Gordie rubbed somebody's face into the ice pretty good with that famous elbow of his. And then late in one of the games in Russia, Bobby Hull scored a goal and the clock just went dark. They usually have the last seconds up there, but suddenly they didn't. It just went dark and somehow the goal was disallowed.

MY ROOMMATE OVERSEAS was the great hockey writer Red Fisher, who was working in those days for the *Montreal Star* (when the *Star* folded in 1979, he moved over to the *Montreal Gazette*). We had a few adventures together, but we also had to get used to each other.

We were staying in the Rossiya Hotel, the biggest hotel in the old Soviet Union. Spending time with Red was a great education in how sports writers work. He'd be typing away in the room doing a story. I remember walking up to him and picking up one of the pages he'd written and taking a look. He said, "Wait a minute, what do you think you're doing?"

"I just wanted to look at what you're writing."

"Don't do that. If you want to read it, go out and get yourself a newspaper."

"I'm in Moscow and you're here and I can't buy a *Montreal Star* and I just wanted to see what you were writing."

But there was no way he was going to let me do that. So I learned something about Red there—don't ask.

Anyway, we got through the series together and had a great time. And then we were packing up, getting ready to leave Moscow and head for Prague, where Team Canada would play an exhibition game before heading home—the same as the '72 team had.

In those days in Moscow, when you went to your room, there was a uniformed woman sitting at a desk on every floor when you got off the elevator. You couldn't take your room key with you when you left the hotel. You had to leave it with her. And it was a huge key.

They got to know you pretty well, seeing you come and go day after day. If I came back and Red was already in the room, she would just point at the door to let me know that he was in there.

So we were getting ready to go and I said, "You know, Fish, when we leave here I'm taking that key with me. I'm not going to leave it behind. This would make a beautiful souvenir."

"I wouldn't do that," Red said. He was afraid of getting in trouble with the Russians.

We went downstairs to wait for the bus that would take us to the airport. Red and I were standing in the lobby of the biggest hotel in Russia. I said to him, "I've got the key in my bag. No one is going to mind."

The next thing I knew, way over there across the lobby was the woman who'd been on our floor, along with two or three army guys—and they were coming straight at Red and me. I said, "I think we're in trouble, Fish." Sure enough, they came to me and pointed at me. "Key! Key! Key!" I opened the bag and gave them the key and it was all over and thank God they let us go.

I don't think Red enjoyed that much—but he found a way to get even.

We left Moscow and went straight to Prague. But before we get to that, I have to explain a couple of things.

My favourite drink is Captain Morgan Dark rum and Coke. Has been for as long as I can remember. Not any other kind of rum—and not any other kind of Captain Morgan. Has to be that one. And not Pepsi. It has to be Coke. Everyone who knows me knows all about that.

So going to Russia, I had to make some preparations. A guy who was the brother of someone I knew from the curling club in St. John's worked at the Canadian embassy in Moscow. He hooked me up in '72 and '74 with a supply of Coke. You couldn't get Coke over there. He'd come over to the hotel with it stashed in the pockets of his trench coat, like in the movies. But not very much of it. We had to have things planned perfectly. I brought my own little stash of Captain Morgan, just enough so that I could have little nips of it over the two weeks, with just enough Coke to get me by.

So Fish and I got to the hotel room in Prague and everything was nice. What a breath of fresh air after being in Moscow. It just felt more free. I decided that to celebrate, I was going to have my last drink. I had an ounce and a half of rum left and one can of Coke.

I got the can of Coke out and Fish went to his suitcase and came back with something in his hand. Then he picked up my Coke. (He's got all of this on tape, by the way. He wanted to remember what I sounded like. . . .)

"Hey, wait a minute! What are you doing with my Coke?"

"I've got a terrible headache. I need it to take an Aspirin."

"Fish, you can't take that Coke. That's the last Coke I have. I've got one more drink. I'm going to sit down and listen to the music and have one more drink."

"But I have to take an Aspirin."

"I'll give you anything you want but not the Coke."

"I've got this terrible headache."

"Well, drink the water."

"I can't drink the water over here."

"I can't give you the Coke."

Then he stood there and dressed me down and gave me the greatest speech in the world about how we'd been together for so long helping each other all the way and now he had a terrible headache and I wouldn't give him my last bit of Coke.

"Can't do it, Red," I said.

"Well, good for you," Red said. "I admire that."

And that was it.

Except that he's still telling people that story, all these years later. Can you believe this guy?

TWO YEARS LATER, I was back calling international hockey again, though this time it was different. For one thing, I was working on the television instead of radio broadcast of Super Series '76. And the series itself was different from anything we'd seen before. Instead of national teams playing exhibition games, this time it would be club teams playing against each other right in the middle of the season, when everyone was in shape and the playing field was level (except for the fact that all the games were taking place in North America, and not on the larger international ice surfaces). The two visiting teams were Soviet Red Army, who were the best in their league—most of the players on the Soviet national team played for them—and the Soviet Wings.

Everybody talks about the New Year's Eve game between the Montreal Canadiens and the Red Army—some people call it the greatest game ever played. That was Danny Gallivan's game to call, of course, and he did a wonderful job. It was an exciting game all right, but only because Vladislav Tretiak stood on his head. The Canadiens actually far outplayed the Soviets that night.

I called the first and the last Red Army games. The first one, nobody much remembers. The Russians went into Madison Square Garden and beat the Rangers 7–3. The last game, though, was one of the most memorable I've ever called. By then, the Wings had won three of their four games (they lost to the Buffalo Sabres) and the Red Army had beaten New York and Boston and tied with Montreal. So once again, the same as in '72, there was a sense that we were losing control. All that was left was a game between the Red Army and the Philadelphia Flyers in the old Spectrum. The Broad Street Bullies, defending two-time

Stanley Cup champions, against the Soviets, with the NHL's pride at stake.

Everybody knows that those Flyers were a tough team who loved to fight, but they had some great skill players as well—Reggie Leach, Rick MacLeish, and Bobby Clarke. Of course, the Soviets remembered Clarke because he broke Valeri Kharlamov's ankle with a slash during the '72 Summit Series.

It was the first period, and there was still no score in the game. It seemed like everybody on the Flyers was hitting everyone on the Red Army. Even Bill Barber threw a couple of hits, and he never did that. Freddie Shero, the Flyers coach, must have said, guys, here's what we're going to do off the get-go. He must have. They hit everything that was moving.

Then Ed Van Impe, who was one of their real tough guys, came out of the penalty box and hit Kharlamov and that was it. Kharlamov stayed down for a long time, but no penalty was called. Lloyd Gilmour was refereeing the game—that was the last game of his career, as he retired. (He gave me his referee's sweater after the game as a souvenir. I still have it. Now, he was always a character and you never knew what he was up to. I remember I phoned him up later and said, "Are you sure that was your sweater?" He said, "Look on the left sleeve. There's a cigarette burn right there." Sure enough, there it was.)

Poor Lloyd. The Soviet bench was going crazy. Finally, the Red Army coach, Konstantin Loktev, ordered his team off the ice.

The broadcast booth in the Spectrum was right behind the benches, down low. I was working with Dick Irvin on that game, and they added Denis Potvin, who had never done any broadcasting before but had played the previous night on Long Island against the Soviet Wings.

No one had ever seen anything like it before. The crowd in the old Spectrum howling and the Red Army players heading for their dressing room in the middle of the period. Dick sensed the moment, too. I heard him say after, "I heard Bob going and I just shut up." I didn't plan it that way, but it turned out to be one of my most memorable lines.

"They're going home. They're going home."

People still remember that call the way they remember "Oh baby!" on the Mario Lemieux goal because I was putting into words what everybody who was watching that game was thinking. We took everything when we played those games over in Russia, and now look at this. The Flyers were hitting them, and they were going home. They kept walking underneath me, with those grim faces. What else are you going to say?

I found out later what was going on downstairs. They had a meeting at the bench, with Aggie Kukulowicz doing the interpreting, and nothing was working. After the Red Army players walked off, the NHL president, Clarence Campbell, got involved, along with the Flyers owner, Ed Snider, and Alan Eagleson, the head of the NHL Players' Association, who'd made the deals to set up those series with the Russians, as well as the Canada Cup. The story was that the players came back only after Eagleson and Snider threatened not to pay them for the series.

Finally, they did come back, and the Flyers manhandled them, winning the game 4–1. Joe Watson, who almost never scored, somehow got a short-handed goal. Philadelphia was the only

NHL team ever to beat the Red Army, and boy, did it feel good.

We went over to our hotel after the game—it was the Hilton right across the parking lot from the rink. It was a big day, and we were all having a few drinks. Roger Doucet was there with us—the famous anthem singer from the Montreal Forum. They'd brought him down to perform "O Canada." And I got Roger Doucet up singing the anthem in the bar. Everybody shut up and he was giving 'er. What a moment that was. And then I taught Roger the words to "Ode to Newfoundland"—which is like our national anthem on the island. "Let's do it, Bob," he said, and then he got up and sang the ode—the first verse and last verse, just like the kids did in school in Newfoundland. Jeez, it was funny.

Roger was one of my favourite guys. He was a lot of fun. And it was always special when he sang that anthem. If you heard him do "O Canada" you'd never forget it.

All those sounds—like the sound of Roger Doucet's voice—are a big part of the character of the game.

12

GETTING THE
NAMES RIGHT

Bill Ryan is a good friend of mine. Growing up we did every-thing together—we went to the same school, played hockey on the frozen pond at Quidi Vidi and we sang in the boys choir at St. Thomas' Church. He's a year younger than me and I always kind of looked after him when we were kids.

In 1976 I was doing television play-by-play of the first game of the 1976 Super Series, between the Rangers and the Red Army. So I was going to New York and Bill had never been there in his life. This was the big time, and I invited him to come and stay with me at the old Statler Hilton near Madison Square Garden and watch the game. After the Russians and the New York Rangers had their morning skate, Bill and I went across the street to Toots Shor's famous bar. That would have been his "new" bar. His old bar was downtown in New York. We went in for lunch and a beer, but really we went in just to be able to say that we'd been to Toots Shor's. Toots Shor was a famous entrepreneur in New York. Anybody who was anything in show business treasured their friendship with Toots Shor.

We sat in the booth and looked around and hardly anyone was in there. But there was an older gentleman over at the end of the bar. He had a cane, and he was sitting there talking to the bartenders. He looked familiar. When the bartender came over to serve us, I asked him, "Is that Toots Shor?"

"Yeah, that's Mr. Shor."

"Well, I'd like to buy him a drink."

The bartender came back and told us that Toots didn't want anything to drink. But then Toots came over and asked if he could join us. He sat down in the booth with my friend and me and I'll bet we talked for two hours. It might have been the most interesting two hours I've ever spent. Everybody knew Toots Shor. Toots used to say, "Bing Crosby and I would go to mass at St. Patrick's Cathedral on Sunday and we'd have a bet. I would bet him that more people would say, 'Hello, Toots' than would say, 'Hello, Bing'—and I never lost." So he was a famous guy in New York in those days. Ed Sullivan used to introduce him—"In the audience tonight, Toots Shor!"—and he'd stand up and take a bow. All the big stars knew him. So this is a great bonus for us.

I got to asking him questions. I had just finished reading the book *The Last Testament of Lucky Luciano*. "Did you know Lucky Luciano?"

Toots looked at my friend Bill. "Your friend he's asking me, did I know Lucky?"

"Was that book accurate?"

"Everything in it was accurate," he said. "There were a couple of little mistakes in it, but it was pretty good."

Now I'm in business. So I asked him about Babe Ruth.

"When Babe and his buddies came into the bar he'd knock off a bottle of rye and then hit three out the next afternoon up at the stadium. He was a good customer."

On the weekends, he said, the mobsters would come in and most of them were packing a rod, but they were all good friends. It was quite a conversation. Then I asked him about Frank Sinatra.

I love Frank Sinatra. I think he was the greatest singer of the twentieth century. The satellite radio in my car is set to the Seriously Sinatra channel, and it stays there. I guess it goes back to the deejay shifts I did at VOCM, and playing his records. If you pay attention to Sinatra's singing, his diction is perfect. There's not a word in any song he sings where you can't hear every syllable. His breathing is outstanding and his timing is top of the line. Everything about him was so good. The orchestra would go nuts when he walked into the room ready to go for a recording session—they all had to be ready when he walked in. One take is what he preferred. And they all got a kick out of his improvising as he'd go along with the beat. He never missed a beat. That's what got me tuned in to Sinatra. The closest I can find to Sinatra now is Vic Damone—and Sinatra himself always said that Vic Damone had the best set of pipes in the business.

So naturally, I asked Toots Shor about Sinatra. I remember he called him "Sinat."

"Sinat did a big favour for me," he said.

Then he told the story. His old bar downtown was in trouble financially with the taxes. It looked like they were going to lose it.

And Sinatra came in and said, there's no way Toots Shor is losing this bar. So he got Dean Martin and Sammy Davis Jr. to help. Toots had three floors at his bar and they each took one for a week. So for three weeks the bar was sold out. Toots made a fortune. Paid off all his debts. Refinanced the whole thing. And he built the new bar we were sitting in now.

And then he told me, "If you ever get a chance to get close to Sinatra and meet him (it's tough to meet him, by the way—he's always got a bodyguard with him), you should call him by this nickname. I'm the only one who uses this nickname on Sinatra."

Now move ahead a few years.

Irving Grundman was the general manager of the Montreal Canadiens. One day I was at the airport in Montreal, flying in from somewhere, and I ran into him and he offered me a ride downtown in his limo. That's when he asked me if I could do him a favour.

"I'd love to have a big lobster party," he said. "Can you bring me back a bunch of live lobsters when you fly in from Newfoundland?"

Sure, I can manage that. So I got the lobsters all packaged up and brought them to the Montreal Forum. Irv had a great time.

"Any time you need anything," he said, "just give me a call."

Later that year I was in Chicago doing a Sunday night hockey game on CBC Radio. After the game we were in the dining area of the hotel and these ladies sitting next to us were all agog over the concert they'd seen that night. I thought I heard them say it was Frank Sinatra. I called out to them and said, "Did I hear you say you saw Frank Sinatra's concert?" "Oh yes, he had a concert here tonight. He's going to Canada after this."

Oh my. I've got to get in on this. I've never had the chance to see Sinatra in person before. So I made a couple of quick calls and sure enough he was going to Toronto after Chicago and then he'd be playing the Montreal Forum.

I didn't waste any time. I phoned Irv Grundman from my hotel room.

"Irv, it's Bob Cole. I'm in Chicago. You told me one time that if I ever needed anything I should give you a call. . . ."

"Okay," he said, "good enough, but please don't ask me for tickets to the Sinatra concert. It's sold out."

"I'm not going to ask you for tickets," I said. "I'm going to ask you for *one* ticket."

He laughed and he said all right and he got me a ticket. It was a great ticket—on the floor on the aisle about ten or fifteen rows back from the stage, which was at centre ice in the Forum. The stage was square with a microphone in each corner and the orchestra pit in the centre—it was Frank De Vol's orchestra.

It was heaven. Sinatra came onstage and he was going from mike to mike and the Forum was full, of course, upper deck and everything. I was sitting there watching the concert of my life.

Well, the concert was over and there were two ladies sitting next to me and they were going crazy all night—understandably. It was an incredible show. Frank Sinatra walked down off the stage. He had a nice soft towel so he could dry himself off. He put on a great show. Top-notch performance. Encores. Marvellous. He came down the steps and he walked down the aisle toward the executive rooms right behind me, next to the Montreal Canadiens dressing room. That was his dressing room.

But then he stopped right at my row. He looked at me. I hate to say it, but I almost passed out. And the lady sitting beside me, she reached across her friend and me and Frank shook her hand. And then the other lady did the same thing and they were both screaming and hollering.

And I was frozen.

I was trying to remember that nickname for Sinatra that Toots Shor told me. But I couldn't do it. I couldn't remember it. I had a great opportunity. I'm sure he would have said something to me. Maybe he would have invited me to come in and have a Jack Daniels with him or something.

But I blew it. He walked on to his dressing room, and I didn't say a thing.

I'VE ALWAYS HAD a bit of a thing about pronouncing players' names properly—and not just with the Russians during the '72 Summit Series. I think it's important to get it right, to pronounce guys' names the way they want them pronounced. It's amazing how often that hasn't been the case. There have been a bunch of times when I found out that everyone was saying a player's name wrong, and I changed it—even if sometimes that rubbed a few people the wrong way at first.

I remember in my early days broadcasting the NHL, I was going to be doing a Sunday night game between the Rangers and the Montreal Canadiens. The night before, the same two teams were playing at the Montreal Forum. Emile Francis was the Rangers coach in those days, and he invited me to fly back to New York with the team on their charter.

So I was sitting up in the front of the plane with Frank Paice, who was the team trainer. He said, "We have a guy on this team whose name you announcers haven't been pronouncing right. Walter Tkaczuk. It's not Tay-chuk, the way you guys say it. It's pronounced Ka-*chook*."

Are you kidding me? That was the first I'd ever heard that.

At the rink the next day I made a point of finding Walt, and he said that yes, it was pronounced Ka-*chook*.

"But that's okay," he said. "I don't mind."

I told him that from now on we were going to get it right—or at least I was going to get it right. I changed it on the radio broadcast that night. But it took a while before everybody else came around, though eventually they did.

I learned a lesson from that. From now on, if I had any question about how a guy's name should be pronounced, I'd ask him. Never mind coaches or other broadcasters. Go to the guy himself and ask him how his parents pronounce it. If your parents say it one way, that's what we're going to do.

I REMEMBER A GAME at the old arena in Winnipeg—the Canucks were in town to play the Jets. It was about six o'clock on a Sunday evening, and the guys were getting their sticks ready for the game. We were talking to Gino Odjick—he was a tough guy who played for the Canucks.

Gino looked at me and said, "You know, Bob, my name is not pronounced Aw-jick. They've been calling me Aw-jick since I came into the league. It's supposed to be pronounced Oh-jick. But everybody calls me Aw-jick."

"Gino," I told him, "we're not going to do that tonight. Let's get it right."

Then I came up with a plan.

"Here's how we're going to do it. You're either going to get an assist or a goal or a frigging penalty tonight for sure. And the PA announcer is going to say your name. Now, I'm going to see the announcer upstairs before the game where they have the meal. I don't know him, but I'll find him and I'll tell him about our conversation.

"His station is down by the penalty box. That's where he does the announcing. And I'm broadcasting from right above the penalty box in that building. You come over to the penalty box before the game and talk to him when he's putting his books and papers together. He'll tell you that I was just talking to him upstairs, and you'll get things straightened out. When it's all set, you two look up at me in the booth and give me the thumbs-up and I'll know that he's got it right."

So I met the PA guy before the game and said, "Now listen, we've got to do this right." He said, "It's been Aw-jick ever since he came into the league." But I told him, "That's not right. So we're going to go with Oh-jick. He'll come over and talk to you about it before the game."

Sure enough, Gino came over to talk to the guy and they gave me the thumbs-up. For me, and the hockey world, it's been Gino Oh-jick ever since.

SOME FUNNY STUFF has happened when I've tried to get the right pronunciation of players' names.

I had called games with Sergei Makarov when he was playing for the old Soviet Union, and his name was always *Mack*-a-rov. But then he came over to play in the NHL and somehow it became Ma-*kar*-ov—they didn't stress the right syllable. So I wanted to get to the bottom of that. He was playing for the Calgary Flames, and after a morning skate I went into their dressing room looking for him.

His English was pretty good by then. I told him that I remembered when he first came over it was *Mack*-a-rov, and now people were saying Ma-*kar*-ov. Which was right? It couldn't be both.

"*Mack*-a-rov," he said. "*Mack*-a-rov is fine."

The other players were listening to this conversation as they were getting dressed. And as I was about to leave, a voice piped up from a corner of the dressing room.

"Hey, Bob, don't forget—it's pronounced Otto. . . ."

Yep, it was Joel Otto, getting a kick out of all this.

ANOTHER TIME, IN WINNIPEG with the new Jets, I was talking to their coach, Paul Maurice, about how you pronounced their goalie's name. He was Ondrej Pavelec. But was Pavelec pronounced like it had three syllables, or two?

"I'm not really sure," Paul said. "Let me go in and ask him."

Paul came out of the dressing room and said, "He's tough to understand, but I think it's three."

"Let me go in and ask him myself," I said.

So in I went and found him and said, "Ondrej, how do you really say that last name? Is it Pav-lek or Pav-a-lek?"

He hemmed and hawed, so I said, "Put it this way. What does your mother call you?"

"My mom?"

"Yeah, what does she call you?"

"Ondrej," he said.

THE THING IS, the players will allow their names to get changed and won't say anything about it unless you ask them. That's why it's Ko-ma-rov instead of Kaw-ma-rov and Goo-stav-son instead of Gus-tav-son. It's awful.

Now they're saying Pa-*ree*-zee—Zach Pa-*ree*-zee. I introduced myself to Zach and we had a great chat. I told him that I knew his dad, J.P. Parise (Pa-ree-zay), a little bit and called his games. "Now everybody has gone to Pa-*ree*-zee, and they tell me that's the way you want it. I don't think your dad would like that."

"I would rather do it his way," Zach told me.

I asked him if he was sure about that, and he was. So that's what we're doing, no matter what anyone else does. I always say to the player, they're going to come to you and you've got to back me up. They always do.

I've been criticized by other broadcasters for it maybe. But that's the way it should be, and for me that's the way it is.

13

HOCKEY NIGHT

I came home from the '72 Summit Series and found out that my work there had received a lot of ink, apparently. I wasn't that well known before that, even though I did the Sunday night radio games and the playoffs. But when I got back from Russia I got a call from Ralph Mellanby, who was the producer of *Hockey Night in Canada*. He said, "We'd like you to think about coming with us and doing some television. How would you like to do that?" Well, that's kind of unreal, but I'll try.

It wasn't the first time someone had offered me television work. I had talked to those expansion teams back in 1969. And then there were a couple more times when I came close to taking different jobs.

In 1970 I got a call from Punch Imlach. The league had awarded an expansion team to Buffalo and Punch was going to be running it. He wanted me to come there and take the television job for the Sabres. We got talking, and he told me how much he was going to pay me and it was good money. I said, "Now, are you sure?" "Yes," Punch said, "you're the guy we want. It's your job if you want it."

So then I began asking him questions, starting with what the length of my year would be. My kids were young then and I was thinking about them. Punch said that I would get two weeks' paid holidays. Two weeks? What would I do all summer? He said that they'd want me to get involved in ticket sales and this and that. Holy cow. That wasn't what I had in mind. I didn't want to sound selfish—who did I think I was?—but I wasn't going to take it. I phoned Punch and thanked him but didn't take the job. And the job was then taken by Ted Darling, who had been hosting games in Montreal. He moved in and did a great job there for years. They had some exciting teams in Buffalo with Gilbert Perreault and Rick Martin.

Vancouver came into the league the same year as Buffalo, and there was some talk that the CBC wanted me to go out there and call the games. But then they decided to hire the local guy, Jim Robson, who had been calling WHL games, and I would stay where I was.

A year later, I got a phone call from WGN in Chicago—the superstation, the biggest television station in America—and they told me point-blank they were offering me the chance to do the Chicago Black Hawks games. The Black Hawks hadn't been on television up to that point because the owner, Bill Wirtz, always thought it would cost him ticket sales. I had actually written him one time about that and said that I thought he was making a mistake. If you put your games on television, more and more people would become interested, and if the job was done properly you'd get more people coming into the building. He wasn't interested then, but I guess Mr. Wirtz finally figured that out for himself and decided that I was going to be the guy to do the broadcasts.

I'd have to move to Chicago and they would pay me fifty thousand a year—which was pretty good money in 1971. In addition to the hockey games, they wanted me to do three innings of Cubs games with the legendary Harry Caray. So innings four, five, and six, plus all the hockey. And I turned it down.

You know why? I hadn't been married all that long. I had two children. I thought it sounded like I'd have only two weeks off a year and I'd be living in the airport, with baseball road trips and hockey road trips. I got cold feet and said no—though I'll tell you, I wondered at the time whether it was the right decision.

I know now that it was. My young family was more important to me than the job or the money.

BUT *HOCKEY NIGHT IN CANADA*? The job Foster Hewitt did, and Danny Gallivan? Well, that was something else again.

When Ralph Mellanby called me, he said, "We have the Hewitts"—Foster, who was still doing radio, and his son, Bill, who had taken over for him on television—"in Toronto and Danny Gallivan in Montreal. But we're *Hockey Night in Canada*. So we could put you in Ottawa and have you travel from there. It would be kind of neutral territory." (Remember, they didn't have the Senators yet.) They would still have to decide how many television games I was going to get. At that point I was still doing the Sunday night games on CBC Radio, and I'd keep doing them until Nancy Lee came in to run CBC Sports and got rid of them in 1976. After that, I was filling in on television games when they needed me, and during the week I was doing my broadcast work back in Newfoundland, reading the news and hosting the Newfoundland version of *Reach for the Top*, the high school quiz show. (I finally left CBC St. John's in 1978 after fourteen years and took a position with the provincial government. Frank Moores was the premier then, and he had created a department to help people deal with the bureaucracy and cut through the red tape. I worked as part of that until 1981, when Brian Peckford was premier and decided to get rid of that department. He invited me to stay on in another capacity, but I declined. That's when I joined *Hockey Night in Canada* full time.)

I didn't see any big need to leave Newfoundland, and in the end it just happened that they left me there—it meant that I could still be the neutral guy, not from Toronto or Montreal or any other NHL city. I wouldn't be affiliated with a team. It just kept going along that way, and it still does. I don't really mind the travel, even though it's a minimum three-hour flight to just about anywhere from St. John's—and with our weather, it can be a bit of a crapshoot getting in and out. I loved the flying. Back then the captain would see me on board and call me up front. It was great. I got to sit in the jump seat lots of times flying all over the country.

For a few seasons there, I would do the odd game on television in addition to doing a lot of the games on radio. But the guys in Montreal and Toronto were so established, there wasn't any real opportunity to do more television than that, and I wasn't interested in trying to push somebody out of his job.

Of course, Danny Gallivan was the man in Montreal. He had it as part of his contract that he'd be involved in the broadcast of any Canadiens game on television or radio, even if they brought in someone else to do the radio play-by-play. So that's how we came to work together. I remember the first game I did with him, which was a nervous time for me—it was *Danny Gallivan*, after all. We were in the old Boston Garden. I was doing the play-by-play and he was doing the colour. He climbed down into that basket-type area where they did the broadcast booth, and now here I was working with one of the legends of the business. Here I was sitting down and Danny Gallivan was saying, "And now here's Bob Cole. . . ." What is that? That's crazy. I guess I've made it. Here's Danny Gallivan introducing me.

We had met. We knew each other. But now he was saying to me, "This is your game tonight. How would you like me to work with you? What would you like me to do?" What would I like Danny Gallivan to do??? Of course I said, "Whatever you want." He was a fabulous professional. Put me at ease right away and complimented me during commercials. He was just a wonderful, wonderful person to be working with. He took me out to dinner afterwards in Boston. It was grand.

I was always a hero-worshipper, and Danny Gallivan was one of my heroes. I will always remember him doing Wednesday and Saturday night games with Dick Irvin. It was fabulous. There will never be another Danny. There was that personal touch of his, his style, his sound. His feeling about what he was doing. You could tell he was into it.

They're still playing that famous clip of his: "Lafleur coming out rather gingerly on the right side. . . ." Just listen to that. You can *feel* the game.

Danny told me that he would grab a dictionary and find a word and practise that word and then throw it into the game somewhere. He really did that. He would find a word in the dictionary and then think of where he could use it. "Sagacious" would turn into "sagaciously stopped the puck." He worked at it. He was a student of the English language and he perfected it.

Outside the booth, Danny had his own way of doing things. I'm not privy to how he prepared for games, but I don't think he spent much time at the morning skates. That wasn't his bag. And he rarely, if ever, went into the Canadiens dressing room. I think he was trying to make sure that he didn't get too close to the players, to the point where that could affect him while calling a game. You feel sorry for a team that's losing, and jeez, you had a great talk with that guy this morning. You become part of it. That's hard to avoid.

A few years after that first game we worked together, we were in St. Louis doing a game—the Canadiens were playing the Blues in the Stanley Cup final. Danny was television and I was radio, and we got together after the game in the Canadiens' hospitality suite. The place was crowded, so we sat down on the floor with our backs against the wall and had a drink of rum. I was in heaven, sitting there with Danny Gallivan. Look at me. I'm here with the best. Danny said to me, "I have a feeling that you're being groomed to take over this job of hockey play-by-play on television."

I said, "Wait a minute, Danny, I'm going to tell you something. If ever that was asked of me and you were still working, I would say no. I would never do that."

"You mean that, don't you?" Danny said. Oh yes. Don't you ever worry about that with me. I'm going to do as well as I can but I would never, never think about that.

We had a great night—the two of us—sipping on our rum.

AS IT TURNED OUT, my big break in television wasn't going to come in Montreal, in any case. It would come in Toronto, under some pretty unusual circumstances.

If you were a fan of the Toronto Maple Leafs, you could have lived your whole life and not heard anyone other than a Hewitt do play-by-play on one of their games. Of course, Foster started way back in the 1920s, first on radio and then on television. In 1958, Foster moved over to do colour on television, while his son, Bill, took over the play-by-play, and then in 1963, Foster went back to radio and Bill worked with different colour guys. When I called the second game of the 1972 Summit Series on radio, they told me that I was the first guy outside of a Hewitt to ever call a game in Maple Leaf Gardens. After that, I did the odd Toronto game on television, but I didn't feel good about it, with Bill still around. That's why I had that conversation with Foster at his eightieth birthday party, where he told me everything was going to be okay.

One night in September 1981, Bill was calling a Leafs pre-season game—Brian McFarlane was his colour man—and something strange happened. Bill had been having issues with his health. He had lost a tremendous amount of weight. That night, he seemed to be disoriented. He couldn't identify the players, and he even called some of them by the names of guys who had retired years before. In his book, Ralph Mellanby said that Bill had a nervous breakdown on the air. I'm not sure if that's what happened, but they did get him out of the booth after the first period, and had Brian take over the play-by-play.

That turned out to be Bill Hewitt's last game. He was never back behind the mike, and they say he never set foot in Maple Leaf Gardens again.

So I got the call to do the next game. They were asking me to become the play-by-play announcer for the Toronto Maple Leafs on *Hockey Night in Canada*.

It was frightening, actually, climbing down into Foster's gondola at the Gardens. I had listened to him broadcasting from there for all those years. I was sitting where he used to sit. It was kind of magic. I was looking down on centre ice and then the game gets going. I'm pretty lucky. This is something I've always wanted to do, and now I get to do it. Not many people arrive at that in their life's work. This is something that I wanted to do forever. I was eleven when I had that knee injury—eleven years old—and pretending to be Foster Hewitt in my bedroom. I didn't even dream about really having the chance to do the same job he did, to work in his famous gondola, to sit in the same chair. Stop it. That's ridiculous. It's impossible. Who do you think you are?

And yet time goes on and it happens and here you are.

I'll tell you, it was scary that first night. How was I going to do this without messing up?

I guess it went pretty well. After the first period they told me that Brian and I had to go on the catwalk up in the rafters outside the booth because they had to put us on camera. People were calling and wanting to know about me, wondering where I came from. They were phoning. The switchboard was going nuts. So we went up between periods. I don't remember exactly what Brian said, but it was something like, "This is Bob Cole, who is going to be with us periodically on *Hockey Night in Canada*. Welcome, Bob. . . ."

After that, I did most of the Leafs games, and it was great. I'm not one to get overly excited, sticking my hand up in the air and saying, I'm here. But now I *was* here, and I get butterflies because of that every night.

EVEN THOUGH I STARTED OUT calling Montreal Canadiens games on the radio, and I've called games for all the Canadian teams over the years, I guess it's true that a lot of people associate me with the Toronto Maple Leafs. After I took over the *Hockey Night in Canada* games from Bill Hewitt in 1981, I became the voice of the Leafs for a lot of folks, which was a great honour, given who had come before me. But unlike the Hewitts, I didn't get the chance to watch a lot of great Toronto teams, and of course I've never seen the Maple Leafs win the Stanley Cup.

In fact, for many of those years, it was the opposite. I saw some pretty terrible teams wearing the Maple Leafs uniform. I remember nights in the Gardens up in the gondola—the cheap seats were behind us, and invariably on a Saturday night the team was losing again and the crowd was chanting, "Boring! Boring!" That sound would come hauntingly down to us with ten or fifteen minutes left in the period. You're trying to sound like it's still a hockey game here, but that chanting was being picked up on our mikes. So we had that for a long time with the Leafs.

But there were some good times, as well. One of my favourites was the unexpected playoff run the Leafs went on in 1987 with John Brophy behind the bench. Broph was one of the real characters of the game—a rough tough guy from Antigonish, Nova Scotia. They say Brophy was the toughest guy ever in the minor leagues. He drew crowds with the way he played in the old Eastern Hockey League. He wasn't that big but everybody feared John Brophy. The Leafs hired him to coach their minor league team, which was in St. Catharines then, and they promoted him to the big club to start the season in 1986 after they fired Dan Maloney.

They had a losing record that year but still scraped into the play-offs in what was a pretty terrible Norris Division. That put them up against St. Louis in the first round, and no one thought they would win. And then a funny thing happened. A lot of Leafs fans were so sure that they were going to lose that they gave up their playoff tickets. They were gone to Florida and this, that, and the other thing. And when the St. Louis series started, it was obvious that all of a sudden the building had become louder than normal. It was explained to me that when a lot of the tickets weren't picked up by the season-ticket holders, I hate to say it, but the real fans finally got the chance to get into Maple Leaf Gardens. Think about all the people in the Toronto area who never had the opportunity to get inside the building. Tickets weren't available even if they could afford them. But win, lose, or draw, Toronto is hockey country, and they were starving for a winner.

Well, here was their chance. They got in and they got the tick-ets and the Leafs put on a show, beating the Blues in the first round.

Brophy had taken to wearing an old-fashioned black fedora behind the bench. Once the Leafs started winning, that became a big deal. They were selling those hats all over the place, and it felt like three-quarters of the building had a black hat on. They called the team Brophy's Boys, and it was exciting. Then, in the second round, they won the first two games in Detroit 4–2 and 7–2 then went up three games to one when Mike Allison scored in overtime in game four. The Gardens went nuts that night.

And, unfortunately, that was it. The Red Wings won the next three to take the series, and Broph was fired two and a half seasons later. He never coached in the NHL again, but he kept coaching in the minors until 2007.

I loved dealing with him. It was a privilege to walk in and have him say, "Come into my office, Coley, and sit down." He intimidated everybody, but we had a great time together. He was fabulous. It was fun with Brophy. He looked so serious but he was always joking.

I remember when Sugar Ray Leonard was fighting Marvelous Marvin Hagler, they had it on closed circuit on the big screen at Maple Leaf Gardens. Broph and I were talking in his office and he said, "What are you doing tonight? We've got the fight here. It's sold out. Come on over—you can get together with us. We're going to have pizza in the office." And then Harold Ballard walked into Broph's office and heard us talking. "I've got a place for you, Robert," he said. "You don't want to hang around with these turkeys."

So that night I sat with Ballard in the front row—that's where I watched the fight. When the prelims were on, some guy came along looking for Harold. He shone the flashlight right in my face and said, "Do you know where Mr. Ballard is sitting?" I said, "Right here next to me." He gave Harold a piece of paper and walked off. "What's that all about?" I asked. "That's the take for tonight." He had it all delivered to him just before the fight. He wanted to know right away how much money he'd made.

THE LEAFS HAD another great run in the early 1990s with Pat Burns as coach, when they got to game seven of the conference final against Wayne Gretzky and the Los Angeles Kings. That final game may have been the most exciting one I ever called in the Gardens outside of the Summit Series.

The Leafs came close. A lot of Toronto fans still believe that Wayne should have been thrown out of the sixth game when he hit Doug Gilmour in the face with a high stick. Then Wayne came back and scored the winner, and he was terrific in game seven—one of the best nights of his career.

I remember talking to Pat about it after. He always figured that if they had made it to the finals, they would have had a real chance to beat the Canadiens. The Montreal–Toronto games were really close that season, and he figured that they had a good handle on the Canadiens. "If only we had a crack at them," Pat said, "we would have had a Montreal–Toronto final." I think there would have been suicides in the country if that had happened. Somebody was going to take it awfully badly if they lost.

ONE MORE THING about Pat Burns—he was the guy who finally got me to quit cigarettes. We both used to smoke. I'd go into his coach's room in Toronto and he'd have an ashtray there waiting for me. Other places we'd have to sneak off and find somewhere to do it. I remember one night when the Leafs were playing in San Jose, some camera picked me up smoking near the coach's room. Someone in a television truck saw it and got security and they told me I had to put out the cigarette and leave the building. Pat was there laughing his head off as I was escorted outside.

Finally, one day in the summer when he was coaching in Boston he called me to say hello. I told him I missed our little get-togethers when we used to have a cigarette and a chat. "I quit that stuff," he said. Get out. "Yeah, I quit smoking." He told me how he met this guy and he tried this anti-smoking stuff and it worked. I didn't believe it. But I got the pills and took one a day and they didn't work at the start, but I kept taking them and one day the craving was just gone. I can't remember to this day when I actually quit, but I had no interest in smoking again.

Later when he was in Toronto, I pulled Pat aside and thanked him for that. He was just about to go out and talk to the media at the pre-game skate.

"At home we call that BBB," I told him—I was talking about the stuff he'd be saying to the reporters to fill up their notebooks and give them clips for the sportscasts. There are more people covering hockey in Toronto than anywhere else in the world, and the coach there has to deal with them just about every day during the season.

"What's that?" Pat asked me. "What's BBB?"

"I'll tell you after."

Off he went. There was a huddle of fifteen or twenty guys waiting and he answered all their questions. When it was done he came back to me.

"Okay, so what was that BBB thing?"

"Bullshit baffles brains," I told him.

The next time we were together, he said, "Here I go—it's BBB time" before he headed out to meet the press. He always called it that after that day.

EVERY ONCE IN A WHILE, somebody asks me about the difference between calling a hockey game on the radio versus doing it on television. Obviously, I've done a whole lot of both over the years. And there is a difference.

I remember once we were doing a game on television from Minnesota, and in the middle of the broadcast we lost the video feed out of the building. They told me, "We've lost video but keep going— we're going to go with audio only." So I kept calling the game.

Not long after that, somebody stopped me at my golf club in St. John's and said, "I've got to ask you something. I was watching that game out of Minnesota when the picture cut out. You changed how you were calling it. You went right into radio mode."

I said, "You son of a gun, you picked that up. That's exactly what I did."

When you call a game on radio, you have to do some of those things that I practiced long before I got into the business. You have to identify players with teams.

It's all right to just say "Doug Gilmour," but if you're not a true hockey fan, and the game is on radio so you can't see, it has to be "Gilmour of the Maple Leafs coming down the wing." You've got to throw that in. I say things like, "He gets to centre ice and nobody left but so and so" or "Cutting down the left side. . . ." On radio you try to paint that picture. Foster told me to practice painting a picture for the person listening. Little things. "They're in the south end to my right and the north end to my left." Automatically, you've got them and they don't even know it. "The Leafs are in their white jerseys and the Canadiens in red. . . ." That kind of stuff. Doing radio you say, "The faceoff is just outside the blue line to the right side of Sawchuk. . . ." You keep that picture going.

That's the difference between radio and TV. Doing TV, you don't try to get everything in. You let it breathe. I could go and do the game and just run every single word together without any kind of swing to it—just words louder and not so loud—but I don't think that's what a TV broadcaster should try to do.

I've had people say to me that they'll be going to the fridge to get a beer, and they can tell by the way my voice is going up that something is happening and they have to get back to the TV. I was taught to do it that way. And I practiced constantly and listened to an awful lot of games. I still ask for an air check of my games and I'll listen to it and check it. I'm satisfied it's still there—the flow. It's not just picking out the players' names and picking out where they're going and the score and how many goals they've gotten so far and how many games they've played without scoring. That's all good stuff, for sure, but sometimes you do that and you miss the flow that's right in front of your eyes. You've got to have that flow. That's what a game should sound like.

I MET KAREN back home in St. John's. We were both part of a crowd going around in the summertime, having a few beers—a good crowd of us having a nice innocent time. Both Karen and I were sports-minded. She played lacrosse in high school at Bishop Strachan in Toronto, where she went for a couple of years. She played basketball at Memorial University in St. John's, and she was always one of the top two or three junior tennis players in Newfoundland growing up. I got her into curling and she got pretty good at the darned thing. She played third stone with me in the Canadian mixed championship in 1973 and then skipped her own Newfoundland team to what was then called the Macdonald Lassie (the national women's championship—it later became the Scotties Tournament of Hearts). And then she went to the mixed again with three other curlers from our club. I didn't go. I was into hockey broadcasting by that time, and it cut into my curling.

We were married in 1966, and even that ended up having something to do with sports. Like a lot of guys of my generation, I've always loved boxing. It goes back to when I was a kid and my dad would let me stay up late on Friday nights and listen to the fights with him. I'll always remember the sound of Don Dunphy's voice, and the clang of the bell.

Over the years, I had a couple of chance encounters with two of the greatest fighters of all time.

When I was a young lad working on the *Fort Amherst*, we docked in New York and I went exploring. I happened upon a pink convertible parked on the street outside Jack Demsey's bar with the word "Sugar" written on the door in beautiful script. Somehow I knew what that meant and I waited, and sure enough, Sugar Ray Robinson came out and got into the car. I introduced myself and had a nice chat with him. What a fighter he was.

Many years later, Karen and I were in London on a stopover, coming back from our honeymoon in Portugal. We were returning from dinner that night and I saw Joe Louis's picture in a window.

"Wait a minute, Karen," I said. "Let's see what this is."

It looked like they were showing films of Joe Louis fights. So I walked in and asked the first guy I saw what was going on. "Oh yes," he said. "We're showing the fight films, and Mr. Louis is here. He's up in the casino. Are you a member?"

"No, I'm just a visitor. But I'd like to go in and see him."

"Well, you have to be a member to do that," he told me. "You're free to go into the auditorium and watch the movies of his fights, but you can't go into the casino unless you're a member."

Well, here I go again.

Karen wasn't interested (can you blame her?) so I brought her back to the hotel and then went back to the place and paid whatever I had to pay to get in and see the films. It was like a movie theatre, but I noticed that over on the far side there was a door that a waiter had been coming in and out of carrying drinks. So I thought, the next time he comes in, I'm nipping over there and getting into that room. That's got to be where the casino is.

Next time he comes in with the tray, I'm booting it in behind him. I get in, and sure enough, it is the casino. Sitting at a blackjack table was a huge man—Joe Louis, one of the greatest world heavy-weight champions ever. He was sitting there and he looked so bored watching all of these gamblers spend their money. He was almost nodding off to sleep. So I went up behind him and I said, "My favourite was the second fight with Billy Conn when you knocked him out in the eighth round. . . ."

He turned around and said, "Wow, man, how are you?"

We had a great chat. I'll never forget how he put out that great big hand to shake mine when I left.

Anyway, I guess it figured that our children would be into sports. Christian was born in 1969, then Hilary in 1972, Megan in 1975, and finally Robbie in 1979. Saturday nights and Sunday nights were special for the family when Dad was doing an NHL game. It wasn't long before the kids were big fans of the game, and they still are today. And they loved skiing. Karen took care of the trips. We went to Gray Rocks in the Laurentians, Mont-Sainte-Anne near Quebec City, Stowe in Vermont, and our own beautiful ski hill, Marble Mountain, just east of Corner Brook. I got into it and had my share of wipeouts. I separated my shoulder twice. But in the end we all became quite proficient.

When each one of the kids was closing in on becoming a teen-ager, I made them a promise. Sometime during the year of their twelfth birthday, they'd get to go on a hockey trip with their dad. Where they went was up to them. I'd get the schedule for the upcoming season and pin it up in my office alongside all the other hockey stuff, and then they'd make their choice.

Christian was first. Her birthday was in November. Somehow she'd become a fan of the Montreal Canadiens. So it was off to Montreal for a Saturday night game. Doug Risebrough was her favourite player, and he was with the Habs then, so I made sure she got the chance to meet him. He was really nice. We arrived in Montreal on Thursday, so there was time for sightseeing in that great city. Because Christian was always interested in horses, we planned a visit to Blue Bonnets race track. We got the royal treatment. We had a supervised tour through the main barn, where all the thoroughbreds were in their stalls. We got to see some serious workouts on the track. It was a perfect afternoon for a young horse-lover. Then came the game on Saturday night at the Forum. It was a wonderful weekend. A little over two years later, Christian attended the tennis program at All-Canadian Academy in London, Ontario. So off she went to a new province and a new high school.

Now Hilary's twelfth birthday was on us. She checked my schedule and settled on a Saturday in Toronto. Why? I thought. She said she wanted to drive down and see her sister in London. It happened that Carling Bassett was playing an exhibition game in London that weekend, so that worked out well. We visited Niagara Falls and then went to the game at Maple Leaf Gardens. Another successful birthday.

Three years went by and my third daughter, Megan, was impatiently waiting for the new season schedule. Megan was always into the arts in school—acting and the theatre—and she went on to great stuff at Ridley College in Ontario, where she and Robbie and Hilary all went to high school. Megan got to be pretty good.

She was the lead in various school plays. She looked at my schedule and saw I had a game in Long Island, New York. Do you think it's possible? I know. New York. So she hit the jackpot and off we go. Manhattan on Thursday, staying in a beautiful hotel. Broadway Thursday night. We saw *A Chorus Line*. This was the big time, for sure. Got a train from Penn Station the next morning to Long Island and got ready for Saturday's game.

My Boy Scout training came in handy on that trip—Megan had beautiful long, dark hair that I fixed into two braids. She sat in the broadcast booth with me during the game. Afterwards, she got to meet a couple of the Islanders players. As we were leaving the Nassau Coliseum, we bumped into the Islanders goalie, Billy Smith, of all people. Well, he was amazing. He took a shine to that little girl I had with me. We had a grand chat. We took pictures. And the evening was complete.

The next time I was around the Islanders I was telling Al Arbour about my trip and how my twelve-year-old met Billy Smith and how great he was. He couldn't believe it. He said Billy Smith talked to nobody after a game—absolutely nobody. So Megan scored big time right there. That was a bit of fun.

Three down and one to go. Now it was Robbie, four years later. He checked the new schedule for 1979. It didn't take him very long. He was looking at it and looking at it and I knew what he was looking for. I had a game in Los Angeles, and this was when Wayne Gretzky was playing for the Kings.

Robbie loved Gretzky. I can tell you a story about that.

One year, Team Canada was playing some exhibition games in Atlantic Canada before the Canada Cup, and Wayne was on the team. They were in Nova Scotia to play a game in Sydney, and the next night they'd be coming to St. John's to play a game at the old Memorial Stadium.

I got word that Gretzky might not play in Newfoundland—Mike Keenan, who was the coach of that team, was planning to rest him. Couldn't have that. So I found out which hotel the team was staying at in Sydney and got Mike on the phone. We always got along well and had a lot of great talks over the years.

I said, "I hear that Wayne might not play in St. John's."

"That's right," Mike told me. "We have to give him a break."

"Mike, you can't do that to me. The whole town is talking about it. Wayne Gretzky is coming to St. John's with Team Canada. What are you doing to me? You've got to play him. I'm pleading with you."

So Mike gave in and said okay, he'd play. And he did—and lit up the place like you wouldn't believe.

At the morning skate before the game, I took my girls and Robbie down to the stadium to watch the guys. Most of the fans were sitting on one side of the building. We came in on the other side and sat there alone. We were behind the glass and Wayne came by and tossed a puck over the glass for Robbie. After the skate I brought Robbie over with me to the Team Canada dressing room.

Robbie was such a polite little guy. Wayne came into the room—it was the first time Robbie had met him—and looked at Robbie and said, "Would you like a pop?"

"No thank you, Mr. Gretzky," Robbie said.

But Wayne insists. "You must want a pop," he says, and then goes back inside the dressing room to get him one. He comes out and hands Robbie a can of Pepsi, and Robbie says, "Thank you, sir."

Now it's two or three years later. I walk into Robbie's bedroom and I see that can on his shelf. It wasn't even opened. He kept that can of Pepsi in his room all that time. He didn't say a word. And there it was.

SO NO SURPRISE that when Robbie saw that game on the schedule, he wanted to go to Los Angeles. I said, "Well, Rob, I see what you're looking at. We'll have to leave early, I guess." It would mean a long time out of school. But we had to do it. I picked him up from school at noon on Wednesday and off we went to California.

Now, somehow Wayne got wind of what was going on, and things started happening. We got first-rate passes for Thursday night's basketball game—Magic Johnson playing for the Lakers. Then we had tickets for the Universal Studios tour where they had the western guys shooting a fellow off a balcony and he falls into a truck. It was a fabulous tour—and Wayne's fingerprints were all over it.

Now it was the morning skate on Saturday and I was at the Forum with Robbie.

Wayne arrived in the private area where he had his parking spot, and he had his daughter Paulina with him. She was only about two and a half years old then (I guess she's kind of famous in her own right now). Wayne's dad, Walter, was on his way out there from Canada, but his flight had been delayed. He was supposed to be at the building to look after Paulina.

Wayne told me, "My dad is delayed—he just called me, he's at the airport, and he'll be a while. Would you look after Paulina while I get ready for the morning skate? Just take her up in the seats and we'll go ahead." I said, this is pretty good. So we had this little baby with us in the stands and pucks were flying everywhere. Talk about a nervous time. Robbie wanted to watch the skate and I wanted to get under the stands to protect the baby. She was sitting on Robbie's lap and every time Wayne skated around that end of the rink, Paulina would yell out "Daddy!" Finally, Walter turned up. So that was a great introduction to Paulina Gretzky.

One of the Kings' PR people came looking for me and told me that Wayne had a stick for Robbie. I got Wayne to sign it and we took a marvellous picture of them together.

As we were doing that, Wayne asked me what time I usually arrived for the game. I told him four-thirty or five. He said Walter would be there, too, and Robbie and I should touch base with him when we got there. So we did, and Walter said we were invited up to the private lounge on the second floor. I didn't know why. But off we go, the three of us.

There was security at the door. We gave him our names and he told us to follow him. We went into this beautiful high-class dining room. It was gorgeous. Had to be places for fifty or so people all laid out with white tablecloths and top-of-the-line everything, and waiters in black tie.

Nobody else was there yet. Just Walter, Robbie, and me. I noticed some name cards on the tables. Robert Wagner and Paul Anka. Movie people and music people. Walter suggested that we just pick a place somewhere and sit down, but I told him, "I don't know about that. This looks kind of organized. Let me check something." So I went up to the head table around where we'd come in. Well, I'll be danged, there they were, the place cards—Mr. Bruce McNall, Mr. Walter

Gretzky, Mr. Bob Cole, Master Robbie Cole. Here we go. So the three of us sat down. And people began coming in almost right away. In came Bruce McNall, the Kings owner, and he took his seat. He was so hospitable, so fabulous to us. He said, "Robbie, they're not here yet, but Van Halen will be sitting just to your left. And for you, Bob, Paul Anka and his wife are right there in front of you." And that's where they were. We were introduced to them and had a wonderful time.

I explained that I couldn't stay long—I had to go to the booth and get ready for the game. And Paul Anka was all into that. I understand you've got to get going, he said. And then Bruce asked me where Robbie would be watching the game. I said, "I've got a ticket for him but I'll find a spot for him up in the booth. There's not a lot of room up there, but it'll be pretty good." And Bruce shot back, "Walter is coming with me in my box. Robbie can join us if you'd like." I looked at Robbie. "Are you okay, Rob?" He said, "Thanks, Mr. McNall" and off he goes with them.

When I got up to the booth I looked down to my left behind the goal, and sure enough there was little Robbie with Bruce McNall.

After the game, Walter brought Robbie over to the booth and we went down to the dressing room. Kelly Hrudey was the goalie then with L.A. He was fabulous with Robbie—he put his mask on him and stuff.

When we were finally getting ready to leave, Wayne said to me, "Mr. Cole"—he always calls me Mr. Cole—"why don't you and Robbie stay over? We're playing the Russians in an exhibition game on Monday night. You can stay at my place."

Whew. I thanked him, of course, but I had to apologize. Robbie had been away from school since Wednesday, and that might not go over well at home. Robbie didn't say a word. That's the honest- to-God truth. Not a word. But four or five years later he said to me, "Dad, I can't believe you didn't take up Wayne on that invite to stay over at his place in Los Angeles." I said, "Robbie, neither can I. I'm so sorry." But the panic was on—he'd been away from school for a week. Sure hope he learned something great at school when he got back!

THIS IS PROBABLY a good place for me to talk a bit more about Wayne Gretzky. I've been lucky enough to call games from the beginning of his career to the end, including all those Stanley Cup wins with the Oilers. I still hear from him every month or so, just calling to check in and see how I'm doing. For me it's a special relationship.

I can still remember seeing him in that little room off the Oilers main dressing room in Northlands Coliseum. It was the place he'd go to be alone for a while before games, and if he saw me he'd always come out and give me a nod and I'd go in and just chat.

Wayne's always been nice like that. Of course, I met Walter and Wayne's late mother, Phyllis. And he introduced me to his grandmother at Maple Leaf Gardens one night. She was there for the game in her wheelchair. His grandmother was the one who used to stickhandle with him on the floor when she'd babysit him. She was the start of it all, really. And he was dying for me to meet her. It was a pretty special moment.

I HAD A LOT OF FUN with those Oilers teams. Glen Sather, who started out as the coach and later became the general manager and the president, is a great buddy of mine—going back to the days when he played with the New York Rangers.

I'll tell you a story. I was in Toronto doing an Oilers game when Wayne was with the team—it was the year before they won their first Stanley Cup. Before the game, I went over to the visitors' dressing room in Maple Leaf Gardens. It was a tiny room. Slats allowed me in while the boys were getting their uniforms and skates on before the morning skate.

Slats and I were talking away and he said, "What do you want from me now?"

"I know you're busy," I said, "but I've got to get your lines and defence pairings."

"Bob, you've got that stuff, haven't you?"

"No, I can't even remember when I last saw you guys play."

Then a voice pipes up behind me.

"It was in Minnesota, Mr. Cole. November 12."

I looked at Slats and Slats looked at me. Was that who I think it was? Here was Wayne with a big smile on his face. And he was right. It was in Minnesota two or three months earlier.

"He knows everything," Slats told me. "He reads six or seven news-papers a day. He knows everything and he remembers everything."

Slats gave me his line combinations and then told me he was busy—he had to give the players a little speech that morning. I joked that I could do it for him if he wasn't feeling up to it.

Well, Slats jumped on that.

"You want to do it?"

He called the players to attention.

"Hold it a minute, everybody. Be quiet."

Wayne was banging his stick on the floor to get their attention, and then everybody started banging their sticks.

"Bob Cole is going to give us our morning talk before the game."

Slats, you son of a gun.

Now the whole room was dead silent and the players were all looking at me.

Slats walked away and left me standing there with the Edmonton Oilers. I had to say something. So I got talking. "I've seen a lot of teams," etc., etc. Oh, the bull I had to get on with. I was scared to death. "I believe what I see here is something that's really looking promising. Things are looking great down the road. Keep working hard. You're going to make it. . . ."

And sure enough, a year later, there it was. The first Stanley Cup.

Slats still remembers that. It was the scariest thing he could have thrown at me. But the guys were great to me. They were all so good and they were all so young.

MOST OF THOSE PLAYERS were still around when I broadcast one of the most memorable series of my career—the 1987 Stanley Cup final between the Oilers and the Philadelphia Flyers. It was spectacular hockey. The Oilers had lost in the playoffs the year before on the Steve Smith play, so they were hungry for another championship, and the Flyers were outstanding that year. Their goalie, Ron Hextall, won the Conn Smythe Trophy as the MVP in the playoffs—only the fourth player in history to win it while playing for the losing side.

It was the first time since 1971 that the final went to seven games, and the atmosphere was electric. There was a friendly competition between the two cities to see which of the two buildings—the Spectrum or Northlands Coliseum—would be the loudest. It was so loud before the games that the anthem singers had to wait for the noise to die down before they started.

I've got a funny story about that.

The Oilers were up 3–1 after the first four games, and so they were coming home to Edmonton with a chance to win the Cup. The noise that night was just nuts. Andy Van Hellemond was the referee, and he and the two linesmen were standing at centre ice, waiting for the anthem to begin.

The anthem singer for the Oilers was a guy named Paul Lorieau. He had a beautiful tenor voice. He sang the solos with his church choir. Paul was a very proper individual. With him, everything had to be classy.

So he was standing down at the end of the rink and the crowd was roaring so loud, he couldn't get started with the anthems. They announced him—"And now, Paul Lorieau . . ."—and it was absolutely deafening.

Then Andy takes off from his spot at centre ice and skates straight down to Paul at the end of the rink, circles around him and then skates back and takes his place at centre ice. Then the anthems finally begin.

After the game I went down to see the guys, as I usually do, and I spotted Paul Lorieau coming down the hall.

"How are you doing, Paul?" I said.

"Fine, fine. . . ."

"You had a tough time out there tonight with the crowd, but you did a great job, as usual."

All he said was, "Under *great* duress."

So now I had to find out what had happened. I went to the referee's room to check in with the officials, because we were all friends. And I said to Andy, "You circled from centre ice and you went in front of Paul Lorieau when the crowd was going nuts. What did you say to him?"

"I said, 'Start singing, or f*&# off,'" Andy said.

He was just having some fun with him, though I'm not sure if Paul appreciated the joke.

So now we're back in Edmonton for the seventh game. Bryan Lewis was refereeing that game. And the crowd is even louder than it was before. So Bryan must have been talking to Andy. With the crowd still roaring, he skates down to Paul Lorieau and circles around him.

After the game, I asked Bryan what he'd said.

"They're here to watch a hockey game, not listen to you," he said. "So, start singing."

Poor Paul. He had an awful time.

I LIKE TO THINK that I made a very small contribution to the Oilers winning the Stanley Cup that year.

I was staying in the same hotel as the team in downtown Philadelphia, and I was standing outside one afternoon passing the time of day and out came Glen Sather. He asked me what I was doing and I said nothing in particular. "C'mon with me," he said. "I've got to line up dinner for the team tomorrow night." Off we go. We walked to this fancy restaurant maybe four or five blocks up. Glen found the manager and talked to him and went through everything. The menu was all set up—it was going to be steak and lobster and everybody would be allowed one glass of wine. The timing was important. They had to be finished by ten-thirty.

We left when everything was arranged and were walking back to our hotel. I said, "Slats, I've got to bring something up. It might not be any of my business, but I've got to mention it anyway."

"What?"

"I'm not saying that the lobster is not going to be fresh. People keep lobsters alive for a long time until they're ready to cook them. But sometimes if fish is just a little off, boy you can get a nasty stomach illness."

(I guess that was the Newfoundlander in me coming out. We know our fish.)

Slats didn't say a word. He just did a one-eighty and we went back to the restaurant and cancelled the whole thing. He wasn't taking any chances.

You've got to be careful with that lobster if it's off a little bit. Could have cost the Oilers the Stanley Cup.

NOW JUMP FORWARD to August 1988. Seeing that date, maybe you know what's coming.

For nine years I hosted a charity golf tournament in St. John's. This was the first one. I invited NHL players, officials, my friends in the media business. And of course, I invited Glen Sather, who was spending the summer at his place in Banff.

The tournament was scheduled for the second Wednesday in August. A few days before that, Glen called me at home.

"Are you sitting down?" he asked.

Well, I guess I'd better sit down.

I'd heard some rumours about a Gretzky trade, with what was going on with Peter Pocklington in Edmonton. But I didn't think it could really happen, until I got that phone call.

"Don't tell me what I think you're going to tell me," I said to Slats. And then he did—and told me I had to keep it quiet. I remember Glen saying to me, "Pocklington's getting a lot of money out of this, but what's the good of money to me?"

It was a terrible thing to do to me. I had the scoop of the year and I had to sleep on it for three or four days before it leaked out. I sat on that and kept my word, but it drove me nuts. I was having nightmares.

Glen said he'd still come to the tournament. But I said, "No, no, you'd better not. Do what you have to do."

The news broke the day before the tournament, while a bunch of the guys were all out having a round of golf. I had Kevin Lowe, Marty McSorley, and Grant Fuhr there. Glen phoned me and said the news had leaked out in Los Angeles, and he was heading back to Edmonton. Later, his secretary, Trish, called and said Glen wanted me to get on the course and tell the boys what was going on—to break the news that Wayne had been traded to L.A. It would be announced that afternoon.

Oh my God, okay. I didn't say anything to anybody. Made sure that there were no TV people around. It was going to be quiet. I got a golf cart and went out on the course. Funnily enough, I met

Grant Fuhr on the sixth hole, a par three, and I pulled him off the fairway. He had hit his drive to the fringe of the green. I told him the news. Fuhr said, "Oh my, I guess I'm going to have to be really good this year." I looked over my shoulder as I drove away and there was Grant holing his putt from about sixty feet. He just knocked it in.

Next I found Kevin Lowe and Marty McSorley. Trish had told me to get Marty to phone Glen right away. "Why does he want me?" Marty asked when I told him. "I don't know, and you're not to talk to anybody until you talk to Glen."

Of course, Marty was included in the trade. He was gone, too. That was an explosive day. Soon the news spread through the whole tournament. Everyone in hockey—and I guess everyone in Canada—was shaken up.

WHEN WORD GOT OUT that National Hockey League players would be competing at the 1998 Olympics in Nagano, we were all excited. All kinds of international competitions featuring the pros had been held since the Summit Series in '72, and I'd been involved in broadcasting a lot of them. But the Olympics were something else—bigger than a Canada Cup or a World Cup. The chance for our best hockey players to compete for an Olympic gold medal was something that every Canadian hockey fan had been dreaming of forever. And now it was going to happen.

Of course, I'd worked at the Olympics before—first in Mexico City in 1968, where there was all that stuff with Bill Toomey and Jesse Owens and Howard Cosell. And then in 1984, the CBC had the rights to the Summer Games in Los Angeles, and they wanted me to be part of the broadcast. In those Games Canada won a whole bunch of medals, in part because the Soviets and their allies boycotted, the same way we'd boycotted the Moscow Olympics in 1980.

They called me a few months before the Summer Games and told me that they wanted me to call volleyball. I tried to talk my way out of it, but they kept calling and eventually I said yes. I talked to one of the producers, finally, and he said, "You're the guy we want. We had a meeting this morning and we want a hockey-sounding, exciting voice to do volleyball." I explained that I'd never called a volleyball game before, but that didn't seem to matter. So I had a crash course in the sport coming up.

Canada had a pretty good shot at winning a medal that year. So off I went to call the volleyball games, which were being played in Long Beach. And jeez, it was magnificent.

That was it for me at the Olympics until fourteen years later, when it was time for Nagano, where I was going to be working with Harry Neale.

Because of the time difference, we wound up doing a lot of games live to tape involving some of the more minor hockey countries—Japan playing France and stuff like that. All told we did fifteen or sixteen games, Harry and I. It felt as though we lived in the rink. Our hotel was close so we walked to the arena every day through all the narrow streets. It was the first time I'd ever seen mirrors on the corners—they were there so you could see a car coming and avoid getting run over. It turned out to be a good idea. Harry and I walked back and forth, back and forth, afternoon and evening. Beyond that we didn't really get a chance to see much of the city other than a couple of days of touring, when we went to the famous shrine called the Zenkoji Temple.

REMEMBER, those Olympics came two years after the World Cup in 1996 where Canada lost to the Americans, so that was going to be the big story. The Russians had always been our number-one rivals in hockey, but a bunch of their best NHL players weren't even going to Nagano because they were in a dispute with their federation. Now the Americans were the bad guys, and they came to Japan with nearly the same team as the one that won in '96. Canada had a great team. Wayne Gretzky was on it, of course, though there was some talk before the tournament that they might not bring him. He was in the middle of what turned out to be his second-to-last season in the NHL, playing for the Rangers—but when I look back at it now, he still had ninety points that year. Canada had Eric Lindros as captain, with Joe Sakic, Steve Yzerman, and Scott Stevens as the alternates. They didn't even give Wayne one of the As to wear. Bobby Clarke was the general manager, working with Bob Gainey and Pierre Gauthier (Marc Crawford and Andy Murray were the coaches), and I think Bobby said at the time that he wanted the young guys on the team to have a young captain. And of course in those days, Lindros was still his guy.

Canada played well from the start. They beat Belarus 5–0, beat Sweden 3–2, and then beat the Americans 4–1 in the last game of the round robin. By finishing first, we got Kazakhstan in the quarter-finals, a pretty easy match, and Canada won that game 4–1. But the big news was in one of the other quarter-finals, where the Americans lost to the Czech Republic 4–1. If the Americans had won that game, as pretty much everyone expected, they would have played Canada for a place in the gold-medal game. Instead, they got beaten—they won only one game in Nagano—mostly because the Czech goalie, Dominik Hasek, was playing out of his mind. When that happened, I think most people in Canada figured it was going to be a cakewalk. Our big rivals were done. Now all we had to do was beat the Czechs, and then probably beat the Russians for the gold. (As you might remember, the Americans didn't take that loss very well. The players went back to the Olympic Village, and some of them trashed their rooms on the way out. It wasn't a good day for the NHL at their first Olympics.)

I guess everybody remembers how that game ended, but what they might not remember is that Canada almost lost it in regulation. There was no score heading into the third period. Canada was dominating, but they couldn't beat Hasek. Then Jiri Slegr put one by Patrick Roy about halfway through the third, and it looked like the Czechs were going to win in regulation. But Trevor Linden scored with Roy on the bench in the final seconds—he took a beautiful pass from Lindros in front of the net and put a shot past Hasek to tie it up. It was a goal we'd still be talking about if the game had ended differently.

Overtime was ten minutes. Canada was playing for the win, but it was pretty obvious that the Czechs were playing for the shootout. We couldn't beat Hasek and they got what they wanted.

So we're going to a shootout and I'm hollering down at the guys in the truck get me the players who are going to be shooting. They finally put up the names on the little monitor we had, and I said to Harry, "This is a joke. Someone is playing games with us. Here we are tighter than drums, and we're getting this. Where's Wayne? He's not here." The list they gave us was Theo Fleury, Ray Bourque, Joe Nieuwendyk, Eric Lindros, and Brendan Shanahan. No Gretzky. The greatest player in hockey, and he wasn't on the list.

"Would somebody stop joking around? I've got to know the shooters." Then I heard a voice in my ear saying, "We're not joking, Bob." Good God. I looked down to the Canadian bench and there Wayne was with his head down. I'll never forget seeing him sitting there, hoping that the guys were going to win. That had to be the worst picture I'd ever seen in hockey—Wayne Gretzky sitting there watching the shootout that they had to win to keep Canada alive, and there was nothing he could do about it. I couldn't believe it.

Hasek stopped Fleury on the first Canada shot. Then Robert Reichel beat Patrick Roy on the first shot for the Czechs and that was it. No one else scored. It was pure agony after that. Poor Wayne. I can still see him sitting there with his chin on the boards while the shootout was going on. Holy mackerel. Unreal. I guess Crawford will never get over making that decision.

Lindros hit the post, I remember, but that's as close as we got. Brendan Shanahan was the last shooter for Canada. I felt so sorry for him. Can you imagine the pressure on the guy?

I remember talking to my daughter Hilary afterwards. She said my call of that last shot was the best call I ever made.

I asked her, "Why is that, Hilary?"

"I could hear your voice saying, '*It's as simple as this. He's got to score. Nothing more to it than that. He's got to score. . . . No.*'

"Dad, when you said 'No' after that pause, we all went 'No.' It was perfect."

It's all about feelings, see. You don't prepare that stuff. When that shot didn't go in, the whole country went "No."

AFTER THAT I called the bronze-medal game, when Team Canada looked like they didn't really care anymore and wound up losing to Finland. I don't remember much about it—and neither does anyone else—which is probably a bit of a blessing.

So now it was on to Salt Lake City, the Olympic Games in 2002—exactly fifty years since Canada had won its last gold medal in hockey—and a lot of things had changed since Nagano. Wayne Gretzky was the general manager this time, working with his friend and former teammate Kevin Lowe, so it was a bit of an Oilers reunion. And they brought in Pat Quinn as the head coach. The pressure to win was tremendous—but it was tremendous for the Americans, too, because they were going to be playing at home. Even after the way the U.S. lost in Nagano, they decided to bring most of that team back in 2002. A lot of hockey people thought they were over the hill, and not many liked their chances to win a gold medal.

The fall before was 9/11, so the security for those Games was tighter than it had ever been. You could certainly feel the tension with all of the soldiers around—and on the American side, they were feeling even more patriotic than usual.

Harry and I were given the choice of which hotel we wanted to stay in, and we wound up at a place called the Sleep Inn, which was maybe a quarter of a mile from the hockey rink so we could walk back and forth. The location was fabulous in terms of work, but it meant that we didn't get to see much beyond the rink. The mountains were all around and you could tell it was a beautiful city.

Toward the end of the Olympics I decided I'd try to get downtown and see the famous Mormon Tabernacle. It turned out that the Mormon Tabernacle Choir was doing a concert there, so I went into the office and got myself a ticket for the concert that night. You weren't allowed into the main part of the tabernacle unless you were a member of the church. One of the people in the lineup told me it was easy to become a member—you could sign up and get blessed right away. But I won't go that far to see a concert if I can just buy a ticket.

It was the most marvellous evening I can remember. Even after touring so many places through hockey, it still stands out for me. The choir must have numbered in the hundreds and they were singing in this magnificent building. It was the most emotional evening, more so than any of the symphony orchestras or choirs or the Broadway shows I've seen. This one took the cake.

Afterwards I got correspondence from the Mormons every three or four weeks with a note and a CD. I guess they thought I might sign up. They haven't converted me yet. But that was an evening to remember. The Mormon Tabernacle Choir. It was unreal.

Everyone knows how that Olympic tournament ended, but I'm not sure how many people remember how shaky Team Canada looked at the start. Game one, they walked right in and lost to Sweden 5–2. The tension was high to begin with, and after that game it only got worse. And then we won against Germany but only by a goal so that wasn't very impressive.

I remember bumping into Ken Hitchcock, who was one of the assistant coaches on the team, after an off-day skate. I guess he saw my frightened look—I was concerned that this was going to end soon and we'd be out again. He said, "Coley, I can assure you that we're improving every minute of every day. We're getting better every time. I know we barely won the game over Germany but we're getting better."

Lo and behold, they played the Czech Republic in the next game, the same country that beat us in Nagano, and it finished in a tie—and that's the way they left it in the Olympics. No overtime or shootout unless it was in the medal round.

It was after the Czech game that Wayne held the press conference where he talked about the referee missing a call when Theo Fleury was hit from behind and about how everybody was out to get Canada. He almost made it sound like we were the underdogs in the tournament. It got a lot of press, and I'm pretty sure that was the idea. Wayne knew exactly what he was doing. He was attracting the attention to himself so he could take some of the heat off the team—and it worked.

The tie against the Czechs was enough to get us into the quarter-finals, where we were up against Finland. Another close one, 2–1. Canada was looking okay but not great. In the semi-finals we got a bit of a break. Sweden had been looking really good, and they beat Canada in the opening game, but then they lost to Belarus 4–3 in the quarter-finals on a crazy fluke of a goal. That meant that all Canada had to do to reach the gold-medal game was beat the underdog Belarus, which they did, 7–1. The Americans played a terrific game to beat the Russians in the other semi-final, setting up a dream matchup.

NOW LET ME TELL you a fun story. Everybody knows that a lot of athletes have their superstitions. Well, early in the Olympics I came into the Team Canada dressing room one morning and chatted with this guy and that guy. I was wearing a *Hockey Night in Canada* baseball cap. Joe Sakic came up to me and looked at the cap, and I guess he decided that I didn't have the brim right. So he took it off my head, shaped the curve, and gave it back to me and said, "That looks a little better."

He got a goal in the next game. So now before every game in Salt Lake City, he'd come look for me and, without saying a word, touch my cap and walk away. He wouldn't take it off my head. He'd just touch it and go. That became his thing—"Where's Bob? I've got to touch that cap."

So I was walking into the arena before the gold-medal game with Kevin Lowe. We walked in together and got patted down. The security was heavy. There were two F18s circling overhead and four helicopters hovering over each corner of the building, plus a lot of police cars. Neither of us said a word. Once we were through, Kevin finally broke the silence. "Nervous time, isn't it?" he said. "I'm scared to death," I said. Everybody had butterflies. What a great set-up for the game. And oh yes! I had my cap with me.

But then I had to go and find Joe. I had to go through even more security to get to the Team Canada dressing room. There was

Joe, standing out in the hallway, waiting for me. He touched my cap and that was it.

He was so great that day. It might have been the best game of his life.

INSIDE THE ARENA, the vice president of the United States, Dick Cheney, was there. The crowd was ready to let 'er rip even before the puck dropped.

It finished 5–2 Canada for the gold medal, but we didn't know until there were four minutes left in the third period how this was going to shake out. It was tied 2–2 until Sakic made it 3–2 for Canada late in the second period. Then in the third period it got down to just four minutes left when Jarome Iginla scored to give Canada some breathing room. And Joe got that breakaway goal to make it 5–2 and that was it.

I think a lot of people remember my call of the Sakic goal. It was just what came to me in the moment.

"They've got a break. It's gonna be a break. . . . It is Joe Sakic. SCORES! . . . Jeeeeo . . . Sakic . . . scores! And that makes it 5–2 Canada! Surely, that's gotta be it!"

The Canadians in the crowd started singing "O Canada." Of course, my mind was focused on the gold medal that hadn't been won by Canada in fifty years. And here we were counting down to the end of it. It looked like they were going to hang on to win this.

"They're singing here in Salt Lake City! Now, after fifty years it's time for Canada to stand up and cheer. Stand up and cheer, everybody. The Olympics Salt Lake City 2002 men's ice hockey gold medal . . . Canada!"

Nothing is scripted. You really don't know what you're going to say or how it's going to turn out. But that turned out pretty well I think. I was saying what a lot of people across Canada were feeling.

Three or four days later, when we got home they were still talking about the Olympics and especially that gold-medal game. Prime Minister Jean Chrétien was being interviewed. I heard him say how exciting it was. Then he said, "And at the end they said, 'Stand up and cheer,' so I'll tell you I stood up and I cheered. My wife and I both stood up and cheered." And I thought, I'll be damned. He remembered the words and everything. It was really touching. It kind of blew me away.

Is that the best game I ever called? That's one of the better ones. Yep.

I GUESS NOW I should at least mention the next Olympics in 2006 in Turin, Italy, which were the last ones I worked, though there's not really much to say. That was a nothing tournament for Canada. Awful. There was no excitement. They just couldn't seem to get things going. The crowd wasn't that into it and the team wasn't playing very well. That Olympics came and went, and at least on the hockey side, it was nothing.

It was too bad. When we first heard that we'd be doing it, Harry and I thought it would be great. I had never been to Italy before and neither had he. But hockey seemed to be new to everybody there. Even around the hotel the atmosphere didn't feel hockey-ish. It was hard to explain. Maybe it was because the team wasn't playing well. There weren't many stories about fans sending best wishes from home. The big thing was the mountains and skiing, but that was a long way from where we were. I never even saw the mountains. We didn't go out much. With so many different teams to cover, there's a lot of homework to be done. So that time I didn't even think about going around the city to see what it was like.

The hockey games were played in two different rinks. My daughters Megan and Christian both had jobs with the CBC over there. Christian was up in the mountains with the skiing, and Megan was bringing us our lunch every day at the arena—that was one of her jobs. Canada played one game in the other building and she bumped into Wayne Gretzky there, and he wondered where her dad was. But I was at the other rink. They brought Wayne back as the general manager of that team, and they brought back a lot of the players who'd won the gold medal in Salt Lake City, plus the coach, Pat Quinn, but it sure didn't work out. They finished out of the medals.

FOUR YEARS LATER, in 2010, the Olympics came to Canada. But CBC had lost the broadcast rights to a consortium that was a partnership between CTV and Rogers, so I was shut out. I watched the Games in Vancouver and Whistler from home in Newfoundland. Sure, it was a disappointment not being there, but the other guys did a great job, and it was an exciting tournament with Sidney Crosby and everybody. I thought that Chris Cuthbert did a fine job calling the gold-medal game. I enjoyed watching it. But given the chance, I'd have wanted to be calling that game. And I'm sure when any of the other play-by-play guys have listened to me call an historic game over the years, they wanted to be in my position, too.

I probably won't get the chance to work another Olympics. But I feel blessed to have called so many Team Canada games in international competition. There's nothing like it—hockey and Canada. It's part of what holds this great big country together. When they fly the flag and play "O Canada," it's like everyone is a part of it. I've been very lucky to play a small part in some of those moments. And it's great to know that when people think back to the '72 Summit Series or to the Olympics or the World Cup, in some of those memories they'll hear my voice calling the games.

14

CALLING IT

One Saturday, I was walking to the old Montreal Forum to watch the morning skate, as I always do when I'm calling a game. As I was walking in the doors on Atwater Street, Ronald Corey was coming in at the same time. He was the president of the Montreal Canadiens at the time.

"Bob, have you got a minute?" he asked me.

Well, if the president asks me if I've got a minute, of course I have. I followed him upstairs and he took me into a room off of his office where they had a big model of the new Bell Centre set up that he wanted me to see. They were still two years away from opening the building.

Naturally, I asked him about the broadcast booth—where it was going to be located.

"They tell me it's going to be up at the top," Mr. Corey said. "That's why I asked you to come up. Have you got any ideas about how we should do it?"

To my knowledge, that was the first time anyone had ever asked a broadcaster about how a booth should be designed. I was flattered that he'd asked me. I said that if there was some way, when the roof is on this thing, you could have beams from the ceiling come down to the sides, you could build a nice booth at the bottom of those beams and you'd be as close to the ice as the booth was in the old Forum. And it would be fabulous. Now, I'm not an architect or an engineer, but from a broadcaster's perspective, I thought that would work best.

Two years later I got my first look at the Bell Centre as it was pretty near completion. They were still doing the pipes in the floor. We were wearing hard hats and we were going to be shown around and stuff. I said I knew where I wanted to go. I wanted to go up and see what he'd done with the booth.

And there it was. Exactly what we'd talked about that morning two years before. Big beams coming down from the ceiling and the booth at the bottom of one of them. Perfect.

The new rink opened in March 1996. Every broadcaster today will tell you that the Bell Centre has the best sight lines in the league. That's what Ron Corey put together.

Later that same year I was at home in St. John's when I got the call telling me that I was being given the Foster Hewitt Memorial Award—which meant that I would join the greatest broadcasters in the history of the game in the Hockey Hall of Fame in Toronto. The other inductees that year were Borje Salming, the great Toronto Maple Leafs defenceman; the late Bobby Bauer, who was part of the legendary Kraut Line in Boston;

and Al Arbour, who was a fine player but was inducted as a builder for his work coaching the New York Islanders to four consecutive Stanley Cups.

It was an unreal deal. My first reaction was, I don't deserve this. Why me? I was only doing my job calling hockey games. I had no idea why they would want to nominate me for the Hockey Hall of Fame. I could never understand that. It was quite humbling.

And to win an award named after my idol, and go in with the likes of Al Arbour and Borje Salming, goodness gracious.

Al Arbour was such a superb guy. He would always call me down to his office in the Long Island Coliseum and sit me down and give me the night's lineup. And I called lots of Borje Salming's games, a lot of them when he was the only bright light on some not very good Toronto teams.

The Saturday night before the induction ceremony they had us do the ceremonial opening faceoff at the Gardens. Doug Gilmour was the centre for the Leafs and he gave the puck to me. I felt kind of strange about that, so I handed it to Salming because he was a big Toronto guy. Somebody asked me afterwards why I did that. I just felt—I don't know. It was kind of automatic.

Funny story—a few years later I ran into Borje and asked him if he still had that puck. I was kind of hoping he might give it to me. He said, "No, I gave it to the kids to play with in the driveway and it was lost long ago." "What?"

The ceremony was one of most memorable moments of my life. That was the last year they presented the awards for media at the same ceremony where they honour players in the great hall. Now they do the media part separately during a lunch and only the players get the royal treatment, so I'm lucky that I was the last broadcaster to get that chance.

In my speech, I talked about Foster Hewitt, the story of that first day when I met him in his office and he didn't know me from a hole in the ground and he told me, "I have no doubt you'll be up here someday." I talked about how Foster said that when they tell you the game was great and they don't mention your name, you've done your job. I spoke about how I was fine with that. I couldn't ask for anything more than just to have people enjoy the game.

It was a great moment. I was thinking about growing up pretending I was doing a hockey game, having listened to all those games on radio before TV even came to Newfoundland. I couldn't believe I was in the Hall of Fame speaking to all those people. I always dreamed of just doing a hockey game on the air. And now look at this. I don't know how they chose me, but they did. I'm thankful for that.

There's a tinge of sadness attached to it now. For years Pat Quinn was the chairman of the Hall of Fame, and every year I'd get a letter from him inviting me to the induction ceremonies. Of course, I called lots of games featuring Pat's different teams and he was always one of my favourites. I got along great with Pat. He would always welcome me into his office to just talk hockey. It was a tremendous feeling to have a coach sitting across from you at his desk talking the game like you were teammates. It was a great favour he was doing me.

Then one year I got the invitation—it was a form letter, but Pat signed it himself, and he added a handwritten note that said, "To my favourite play-by-play announcer. I hope you're doing well."

Pat died two weeks after that.

I WANT TO TALK a little bit about some of the medical challenges I've faced over the past few years. For the most part, nobody knows about this other than my family, and I managed to keep working all through it while hardly missing a beat. But I think by telling these stories now it could help people be more aware of circumstances that might seem like nothing to them at the time, but that turn out to be serious. Like a lot of men, I've been remiss all of my life getting things checked, and the truth is, I've been lucky. Maybe after reading this, a few of you will call your doctor and get up to date.

For most of my adult life, I've enjoyed good health. After that period as a boy when I was laid up in bed with the bad knee, I hardly visited a hospital for years, other than to fix up a nose or hand that I might have broken playing hockey.

Then in June 1980, I got what I thought was the flu, with pain in the abdomen that I dealt with for the better part of a month before the doctor decided to bring me into the hospital and do some examining. Sure enough my appendix had ruptured thirty days before and it became retrocecal appendicitis. It had been there for a month and I was very lucky that it didn't break through. They did emergency surgery and I was laid up for three weeks or so, but the hockey season was over, and I was fine for the next few years. But then things started to get a bit more serious, starting in 1997.

The dentist I go to in Toronto is named Dr. Steve Cochran. He's a fabulous guy. One of the finest gentlemen you could ever meet. I was heading up to do a game on a Saturday, and I decided to fly in early, on Thursday, so that I could see Dr. Cochran on the Friday.

The night before the flight I didn't sleep well. I got up in the morning and I wasn't feeling so hot, but I didn't have any idea how bad I really was. Dr. Cochran's assistant Irene called to remind me about the appointment. When she heard my voice she said, "Bob, you don't sound right. Is there something wrong? You don't sound very well. Now don't worry about the appointment. We can get you another one for next week. If you don't feel right you shouldn't get on that airplane."

I reassured her and told her I was fine, but after I hung up, I decided to call my family doctor Pat Dobbin. His wife Joan answered the phone.

"You know Bob, you don't sound so hot," she said.

So now she's the second one to tell me that.

I called another doctor, who was closer to my home in Topsail, Dr. Barry Fraser.

"You don't sound right to me," he said. "Why don't you come up so we can take a look at you."

Jeez, if anybody else says that to me, I'm going to quit.

So I got in the car and drove up and when I got there I couldn't quite remember where Barry's office was. I had to ask somebody. So that wasn't normal.

Barry saw me and said, "Holy cow, you don't look so hot."

He left the examining room for a second—I found out later it was to make a few phone calls. When he came back he said, "You and I are going for a ride. Who can we get to pick up your car? I've got an ambulance coming. We are getting to the hospital right away. We've got people waiting for us."

We got to the hospital and sure enough the cardiac guys were there and I was admitted right away. I was having a heart attack and didn't know anything about it. I just felt a little different, a little off.

It turned out to be a relatively minor thing. All of my medical tests now show no damage to the heart. And I only missed that one Saturday night hockey game. I just kept going.

The following spring, I missed a game during the playoffs, but nobody really knew what happened there. The truth is, I had a minor stroke.

It was in May 1998, the morning after a Saturday night game in Toronto during the playoffs. I got up and looked at myself in the mirror and there was something wrong with my right eye. My vision was okay but the eye was askew, and then I started to feel a bit weak. I phoned my doctor, Pat, back home in Newfoundland and he suggested that I get over to Toronto Western Hospital and talk to somebody in the ophthalmology department.

Now over the years I became great friends with the Toronto Maple Leafs' team doctors—especially the plastic surgeon Dr. Leith Douglas and the orthopedic surgeon Dr. Darrell Ogilvie-Harris. Terrific fellows.

I called Dr. Douglas and told him what had happened and asked him if he knew anybody at Toronto Western. He gave me a couple of names and told me to get over there right away.

I went over in the afternoon about one o'clock and who walked in but Dr. Douglas. What are you doing here on a Sunday? "I've got nothing better to do so I thought I'd just come down," he said. And then he took over, directing everybody.

I was in the hospital for about a week. I missed one playoff hockey game—the first one I ever missed. I got out of there and everything was fine. My vision was fine and I went right back to work and no one was the wiser. It wasn't publicized or anything, so that was good.

A few years later, things got a bit more serious. It was 2003 and I was flying home to St. John's after a Saturday game when I had a strange pain in my back that I'd never had before. I never had any back problems. But I couldn't get comfortable in the seat. I got home and wasn't feeling so hot so I phoned yet another doctor friend of mine, Ron Whelan, head of radiology at St. Clare's Hospital in St. John's, and said I've got this pain in my back and I don't know what the hell it is. I'm going to go to the physiotherapist tomorrow and see what's going on. Ron said I should give him a call after that.

I went over and they twisted and turned and probed around a little bit and they couldn't see anything out of the ordinary so I just let it go. But on the way home I got pinched up in the back again and I could barely get out of the car. To get to bed I had to pull myself up the stairs, one at a time, backwards. It was really bad, so I called the doctor again and went to see him the next morning.

It was getting worse. I got over there and got the x-rays done.

"Okay, you've got a problem," he said. "You've got a herniated disc. But we've got something else in there as well that we had a look at. It looks like you've got an aneurysm developing."

The doctor suggested I take the pictures up to Toronto with me the next time I was doing a game so the medical people there could take a look at them and suggest a course of treatment. Nothing needed to be done right away, but it was something they needed to keep an eye on.

So I put out the word to the Leafs' doctors and I then got a call between periods—there was a doctor waiting to see me at the end of the catwalk. He was nervous about walking across it to get to the broadcast booth. It was Dr. Douglas, and he asked me to come down right away after the game and talk to him—don't go back to the hotel.

When I got there the Leafs' doctors were all gathered and they had the x-rays in front of them. They told me they didn't want me to go home to Newfoundland the next day. Instead, they wanted me to go up to Toronto General and get checked out.

On the Monday morning I got a call to go over and see Dr. Tom Lindsay, who would become a very good friend of mine. He's one of the top vascular surgeons in the country and a marvelous person.

Dr. Lindsay had two or three interns with him and they looked at everything and did their examination. Then he told me more about what's called an abdominal aortic aneurysm. It would grow a certain amount every year, and they'd keep an eye on it, and eventually the time would come to have surgery to take care of it.

That happened in 2004. We were in Tampa calling game seven the night that the Lightning won the Stanley Cup. I got a call from Dr. Lindsay's office asking me to stop in Toronto on the way home to have another scan. (The truth was Dr. Lindsay had already booked the operating room.) When I met him, he leaned back in his chair and said, "We looked at everything. What do you say we go ahead and repair this right now?"

So I called the kids and told them what was going on and they all came out to Toronto. It was going to be a serious operation.

A lot of people who have those kinds of aneurysms don't discover them and if it ruptures, you only have two or three minutes and then you're gone. I was very fortunate, going in about the herniated disc and then having some good doctors around me.

I went in there on June 23—the day before my birthday—and they did the surgery right away. It was pretty heavy.

The morning of the operation the doctor told my kids that they could stay with me until we wheeled up to the green doors of the operating room. As they were taking me in, my daughter Hilary took a loonie covered with tape and secretly stuck it under the table I was on.

So a lucky loonie—just like Wayne Gretzky at the Salt Lake City Olympics.

I was in the hospital for about a week and it took quite a while to get over that. Again, because it happened after the hockey season nobody outside of my family really knew about it.

Talking to the doctors, I found out that one of the things they were trying to do in the vascular area of medicine was get more people to have routine CT scans. It's a simple thing and it's not invasive. It could save a lot of lives.

The doctors asked me if I would help them and so I was interviewed for a story that ran in the *Globe and Mail*—they did a full page on it. I hope it made a difference.

Now, every two or three years I get a reexamination to make sure everything is working—and so far it is.

I had been very lucky a couple of times. And I was about to get lucky again.

Not that long after the aneurysm, Harry Neale and I were in the booth in Toronto getting ready to do a game. The warm up was over and it's fifteen minutes before puck drop and I thought I heard Andy Frost, the announcer at the Air Canada Centre, say something about someone being honoured. I heard applause and I thought I heard the name Dr. Tom Lindsay.

I went down to see Andy and sure enough, that was the case. Every month they recognized someone who had done good work in the community, and on this night it was Dr. Lindsay. Andy showed me where Dr. Lindsay and his wife were sitting to watch the game. I got a note down to him and invited them up to the booth between periods.

They came up during the intermission. Now I have a riser build up where we put our chairs so we can see over the heads of the reporters in the press box in front of us. When Dr. Lindsay and his wife came through the door I got down off the riser, and I had a twinge of pain my right knee. I guess I made a noise, because Dr. Lindsay asked me what was wrong.

"It's nothing," I said. "My right knee gives me trouble now and then. No big deal."

Then we went on with the visit. I let him try on my headset and talk to the truck and he had a ball.

The following Wednesday I got a call at home from Dr. Lindsay, thanking me for the visit.

"Now about your knee," he said. "You looked like you were having a little trouble there. When you're back in Toronto I'm going to have somebody look at it."

So eventually they did some surgery and removed some scar tissue and my god it was perfect, it was great. I went back to see the Leafs' doctors—Dr. Douglas and Dr. Ogilvie-Harris—to have the stitches taken out. They checked the knee and the incision and it all looked just fine. And as they were taking the stitches out they asked me if I had any other health concerns.

"Well," I said, "every once in a while I get a little discomfort down in my abdomen on one side or the other."

They wanted to know when I was scheduled to go home and I told them it was that afternoon. They asked me to hang around a bit longer so they could x-ray my abdomen. They called Dr. Lindsay and he decided to admit me to hospital, put me on antibiotics and then to do some surgery to see what was happening. They had discovered something in there that had to be taken out—a tumor in my colon. And they never would have known about it except for that visit to have the stitches taken out of my knee.

Dr. David Urbach did the surgery. They took out a big piece of my colon where the tumor was—it turned out to be cancer—and checked seventeen lymph nodes, all of which came back clean. My kids came in for the surgery again.

I didn't miss a game. After the surgery they asked me to stick around Toronto for a little bit, so I got a room at the Royal York Hotel. Five days after I got out of the hospital I was calling a game in Ottawa—and then did another one the next afternoon in Montreal. I wasn't really feeling my best, but no one seemed to notice that but me. If I couldn't have done the game, I wouldn't have. But I felt well enough and I was cleared by the medical people, though they were all concerned about it.

One day a few months later, when I was in to see Dr. Lindsay, I bumped into Dr. Urbach who did the cancer surgery. I was delighted to see him.

"I want to say thanks," I said.

"For what Bob?" he asked.

"You saved my life."

He responded simply and with humility: "That's what we do." It just blew me away. It was beautiful.

Reading this will be the first time any of the people I work with will know of these events. I decided to share them now because I am so grateful to those dedicated doctors and nurses who saved my life and allowed me to continue to do the job I love. I have survived a ruptured appendix, a heart attack, a stroke, an aneurysm and cancer. We all have our health challenges. The important thing is to face them and move on.

ON OCTOBER 14, 2006, I was part of a broadcast that made history in Canada. It was a great, historic moment—but like a lot of great, historic moments, it came about by accident.

The *Hockey Night in Canada* crew was set up at the Air Canada Centre in Toronto to do a Saturday night game between the Leafs and the Calgary Flames. I was sitting in the stands for the morning skate, as usual, when Sherali Najak, the senior producer, sat down beside me and told me we had a problem.

Harry Neale was supposed to be working colour with me, but there had been a big snowstorm in the Buffalo area where he lives, and it looked like he wouldn't be able to make it in for the game. We needed to find a replacement fast, and Sherali had an idea.

Cassie Campbell was already working for *Hockey Night* as a reporter, and she was assigned to work the game that night. What would I think about her stepping in and doing the colour with me? He had spoken to Cassie already and she was naturally excited to go ahead, but she was also a little bit nervous. She had done some colour commentary on women's hockey games in the past, but not on an NHL game—never mind on the big national stage on Saturday night.

We sat in the seats and talked about it. "You don't have to do it if you don't feel comfortable," he said. "This is quick notice. We can find somebody else."

I said, no, let me talk to her. She's a great girl. She was captain of the national team and won a gold medal in Salt Lake City. She has lots of experience playing hockey. I think she'll be fine.

Cassie came over and we chatted about everything. Of course she was a bit concerned. Why wouldn't you be?

I said to her, look, you're not going to be as nervous as I was when I did my first game, so don't worry about it. (I found out later that that made her feel great.)

Preparing for the game, I told her she should be up in the booth an hour before the opening face-off. I arrived an hour before and she was already there getting things ready.

I did my best to make her feel at home, and I hope I did. We talked about the broadcast and I told her not to worry about a thing for the first two or three minutes—I'll take care of that and then I'll ask you a nice polite question and it will be right where you want it. It will be perfect, and then off we go.

I think she did a great job. She gave me a great big hug when we were done and told me that it was a wonderful experience.

"We just made history," I said to her.

Later she sent me an autographed picture of the two of us in the booth: "I will never forget October 14, 2006," it read.

On the following Monday, they wrote a story about it in the *Globe and Mail*.

When we do *Hockey Night in Canada* games together now, Cassie always throws it up to the booth introducing me as Mr. Bob Cole—she's the only one that adds the "Mister" part, and does it all the time. It's a lovely, respectful thing to do, and I also think it's a way for her to remember that game we worked together.

IN 2008, things began to change for me at *Hockey Night in Canada*. That is the year they told me that I would no longer be doing the Stanley Cup final. Of course, I wasn't happy. The Stanley Cup final. Are you kidding? I'd been doing play-by-play for forty Stanley Cups.

That spring when the finals were on I went to Florida. Hit a bucket of balls every morning, then another bucket, and kept going. Sorry to say my handicap did not change. As a matter of fact, it may have gotten a little higher. That wasn't easy. It's still not easy. Such is life.

IN 2015, Rogers Sportsnet took over the national television rights for the National Hockey League, including *Hockey Night in Canada*.

I've always worked with short-term contracts. In the early days, and again today, it's year to year and that's fine with me. If I do my job I know I'll be back to sign another one. I've always said, look, I'm going to give it my best shot. Don't worry about that. I love what I'm doing and I'm going to try my best to do it well.

So I've been doing that for fifty years. And I'm happy with it. It was a great vote of confidence when Scott Moore, president of Sportsnet and NHL properties, met with me during the 2015–16 season and told me he would be increasing the number of games I had for that season. I am delighted to still be part of it all. I don't know how many games I've worked, but I think there are some people out there who keep track. And I've worked with a staggering number of different guys in the booth. And I'm happy to keep going.

Retirement? I don't even know what that is. It's a funny word. I've always said that over the years, I've been around people in different parts of the government bureaucracy, of CBC, and there are some people who say they're retiring. "I've got two years and nine months left—and I can't wait." Why would you want to retire when you can walk into the United Center in Chicago, and even if you don't know a lot of the guys, Jonathan Toews comes up to you and says, "Hey, how are you doing, Bob? It's great to see you. We are glad you're here to do our series." It makes you feel part of it all.

So retirement has never entered my mind. Why would I want to retire? I don't know what I'd do. You can't fish salmon for three hundred days a year. Hockey is with me all the time. If I'm not working, I'm home looking at the schedule to see who's playing tonight on TV. It's a big part of my life.

MAYBE I COULD HAVE felt that way about a different career. I could have ended up on the high seas after those two summers when I was a boy and went to work on the ocean liners. At the end of the second summer, I was offered a job— the chief steward asked to see me and I went over to meet with him on a new ship called the *Ocean Monarch*. It was a beautiful ship painted in the Cunard Line colours with the black hull and red-and-white stack. It looked like the *Queen Mary*. It was about to embark on its maiden voyage to the Hawaiian Islands. He wanted me to work that trip, but I figured I'd better finish high school at least, so I went home instead. When you're sixteen or seventeen years old you could easily be captured by an exciting life like that. I might have gone heaven knows where. But instead I decided to head back to St. John's and go back to school, so that was one path not taken.

The other one was flying. I got that scholarship with the Air Cadets, and a little taste of flying was enough to make me want to do it forever. But it didn't come about, for one reason or another. I would have been happy as a pilot. I would have joined the RCAF if they'd been willing to guarantee that I would fly. It would have been a different life and it would have been fine. A pretty exciting life. I could have gone on to get my commercial licence and wound up working for an airline. I guess I'd be retired now. But thank God I'm still working and I love it.

The first radio job was kind of glamorous. That captured my imagination pretty quickly, and the money was better than average for somebody coming out of high school. I thought about university, but radio seemed more appealing to me at the time, and broadcasting hockey games was something I'd always wanted to do. Then being a sportscaster at VOCM, and CBC, and the auditions for the NHL teams that were coming in during the first big expansion. I remember I got letters back from all the new teams—Philadelphia and Minnesota and all those teams that came in. I didn't get those jobs but I was always in the top three—if I had, who knows where I might have wound up. They did offer me the job with the Oakland Seals but I was scared to go that far away. (I made the right decision there, as it turned out. They didn't last very long.) And I was offered a job in Chicago doing baseball and hockey, but I didn't take it because my children were too young to move. I was nervous about the whole thing and didn't do it. More roads not taken.

Finally, *Hockey Night in Canada* came along. It was like a wild dream come true, the dream I had when I was bedridden for all those months as a boy. Hockey was everything to me—listening to the radio, reading about it and pretending I was Foster Hewitt.

And then I got there. I guess that turned out to be a pretty lucky road. And I got to travel it while living at home in Newfoundland, which suited me just fine.

I'VE NEVER THOUGHT about my age. It has never entered into anything I do, at least in terms of my work. I have a routine that I follow strictly, a regimen that I adhere to no matter what's going on. Hockey is very important to me. When I'm asked to do a job, I try to give it my best and I'll continue to do that for as long as I know I can. If it becomes too difficult, I won't enjoy it. Nobody wants that. But I'm still enjoying what I'm doing, and I love meeting the people I do and the young hockey players coming up. I've been through generations of them now. They become good friends. It's a great vocation I have. I earn a half-decent living. And it's the best game in the world. There's nothing better than to be part of it.

The Stanley Cup finals always were a great culmination of a year's work. I miss that part of it. But working all the way through the season up until then, it's still wonderful to be part of it all. When one season ends I look forward to the next.

I still regularly critique my own work the way I always have, watching air checks of games to see how I'm doing. For instance, last season, I got a DVD of the Edmonton game where I met Connor McDavid for the first time in Montreal. I watched that game ten minutes, fifteen minutes, half an hour, an hour maybe at a time. I went through bits and pieces, just listening to it and trying to enjoy it and hoping that it sounded all right, while looking for places where maybe I could have paid more attention to what I was doing. I enjoy that process, too.

And you know what? I don't think I sound any different than I did years ago—at least not that much. It's amazing, really. I've got some old tapes I listen to, and not much has changed in the way I called a game then and the way I call it now. Other people might have a different opinion on that. But it still sounds pretty good to me, and I feel good about that. That's a nice feeling to sit back and say, okay, we're doing all right. Let's keep 'er going.

I'd stop tomorrow if I felt like I wasn't doing the game justice. If a viewer can't enjoy the game the same way I enjoy working it, then something would be amiss. There'd be no point in fighting it.

But when I get in the booth to do a game, I'm still totally involved. I'm a different person. It's my workplace and that's it.

What's the best thing about my job? That's a tough one. Being part of this amazing hockey family and contributing to the public's enjoyment of the game. Having people you've never seen in your life just say hello as you walk by. "I just want to say hello, Mr. Cole. I've been listening to you for a long time. Love listening to you. Keep it up. Please don't retire. I enjoy your work. . . ." Hearing things like that kind of make you sit back and say, wow, I never thought people were thinking like that. It's very rewarding.

And that's part of what keeps me going, part of what makes the game tonight just as important as any of those great games I called in the past. It feels the same to me. Everything is the same. I meet the coaches. I want to see the line combinations and the defence pairings. I've got to be ready.

The faceoff is coming. I wait for the cue, I'm introduced and away we go.

ACKNOWLEDGMENTS

There is simply no way to thank everyone, particularly in a book that covers so many years. I have certainly worked with too many fine people at the CBC over the years to be able to thank them all by name. But to the many friends and professionals who have helped make my job so rewarding, I offer you my heartfelt gratitude. One person I will name, though, is Joseph L. Butler, who owned VOCM in St. John's. If it weren't for him, I would never have got my start on air.

When it comes to putting a book together, a lot of different people are pulling at the oars. Thanks first of all to Stephen Brunt. I couldn't ask for a better writer to help me get my words down on the page, and it didn't hurt that he was willing to do a little fly-fishing as we worked. And thanks as well to editor Nick Garrison, who worked closely with us and so ably steered this book to the finish line.

The project would never have come together if it had not been for my lawyer and friend Pat Gallivan, who was there from our very first meeting with Stephen and Nick in Toronto, through to the very last proofread. Thanks for your careful attention at every step along the way. Finally, I have been lucky to have my children standing by to help with so many of the details as the manuscript came together. As with so many things, you made it all worthwhile.

INDEX